Joke Stew

Other Books by Judy Brown

Joke Soup

Joke Stew

1,349 More Hilarious Servings
from Today's Hottest
Comedians

Edited by
Judy Brown

**Andrews McMeel
Publishing**

Kansas City

For information, write Andrews McMeel Publishing, an Andrews McMeel Universal company, 4520 Main Street, Kansas City, Missouri 64111.

01 02 03 04 RDH 10 9 8 7 6 5 4 3 2

Library of Congress Cataloging-in-Publication Data
Joke stew : 1,349 more hilarious servings from today's hottest comedians / [edited by] Judy Brown.
p. cm.
ISBN 0-7407-0992-5 (pbk.)
1. American wit and humor. I. Brown, Judy.
PN6162 .J57 2000
818'.540208—dc21   00-036178

Book design by Holly Camerlinck

Preface

There was a sea change in American stand-up comedy after World War II, when it truly became a pop-culture art form of merit. Suddenly stand-up transmogrified from the old-fashioned story jokes, the vaudeville and Catskill style, to more of a conversation with the audience about the personal and social concerns of the comedian.

The 1950s (and the beginning of the Civil Rights movement) also saw the first generation of black stand-up comedians, such as Godfrey Cambridge and Bill Cosby, who didn't have to play dumb in order to entertain a mainstream (read: white) audience.

The first female comedians to stand up alone and have fun with the specific concerns of women also debuted in this decade—Phyllis Diller, notably—and opened the door for the outspoken generations of funny females to come.

This was my parents' generation of comics, and I caught the comedy bug from their dedicated interest. I've followed stand-up for more than forty years, and the material in *Joke Stew* (and its predecessor, *Joke Soup*) cover some of this range.

But I've gathered especially from the current, alternative, breaking wave of new, young comedians. As you read this, the air fairly crackles in the comedy clubs and coffeehouses of Los Angeles (and San Francisco and New York and . . .) with the wit of the next generation of comics. This is just a sampling.

Acknowledgments

First and foremost, I'd like to thank the comedians who produced the jokes selected for this volume. I've experienced firsthand the blood, sweat, and laughter involved in carving out truly funny and insightful material, and I give full credit to those whose contributions helped make this a mirthful book.

This includes, of course, my stand-up comedy students. God knows it's sometimes been hard work for us to wrangle those jokes from out of your life experiences. But it's been worth it for me to hear the laughs you get on stage, to see you and some of that same material end up on television and in the movies, and now to see your jokes in print.

I'd also like to thank those behind the curtain who were instrumental in getting this book on the road. That would include my incisive editor, Jean Zevnik; the hardest working woman in contract land, my agent, Carole Bidnick; and my associate Jeannie Dietz, for the hours she devoted to Comedy Central.

(If you're a comedian who would like to be considered for future volumes, or if you'd like to learn the craft of crafting jokes, please contact me at judybrowni@usa.net.)

Accent

I never met anyone who thinks southern is the world's most intelligent-sounding accent. None of us would want to hear our brain surgeon say, "Aright . . . what we gon' do is the saw the top of yer head off, root around in 'er with a stick, and see if we cain't maybe find that dadburned clot." You'd say, "No thanks. I'll just die, okay?"

—*Jeff Foxworthy*

Accident

Ever been stuck behind an accident, and when you finally see the wreckage, you're actually happy? "Things should pick up now, soon as we pass this carnage."

—*Paul Reiser*

I got in a car wreck when I was twenty-two. Hit a damn lake. I thought the road was slick. State trooper sloshing up to my car asks me, "Have you been drinking?" How many sober people do you know who slam into lakes? "No, I ran out of gas. I could have made it across with a full tank."

—*Kenny Rogerson*

My girlfriend just got out of the hospital. She had to have her stomach pumped 'cause I gave her what I thought was cotton candy, but it turned out to be insulation on a stick.

—*Steven Wright*

Adoption

I adopted a baby. I wanted a highway, but it was a lot of red tape.

—*Margaret Smith*

I became a mom six months ago. I adopted a highway. I'm trying to teach it to pick up after itself.

—*Nancy Jo Perdue*

Adultery

It's a good marriage, but I think my wife has been fooling around. Because our parrot keeps saying, "Give it to me hard and fast before my husband, Jonathan Katz, comes home. And, yes, I'd love a cracker."

—*Jonathan Katz*

I discovered my wife in bed with another man and I was crushed. So I said, "Get off of me, you two!"

—*Emo Philips*

Advertising

I saw a subliminal advertising executive. But only for a second.

—*Steven Wright*

The basic beer ad: big-breasted babes in bikinis. Beer won't get you babes. But if you drink enough, you think they're babes. And if you drink more, you grow your own breasts.

—*Norman K.*

A man is paralyzed mentally by a beautiful woman, and advertisers take advantage. Like ads where a woman in the bikini is next to a thirty-two-piece ratchet set. We're going, "Well, she's right next to the ratchet set, and if I had the ratchet set, it would mean that . . . I better just buy the ratchets."

—*Jerry Seinfeld*

Aging

I'm twenty-five now and I'm terrified that time is passing me by. I'm hyperaware of what others have accomplished by my age. My worst tormentors are the Beatles, Mozart, and Macaulay Culkin.

—*Ann Oelschlager*

Just after my thirtieth birthday, instead of growing hair on my head, I now was growing it in places where I didn't need it, like the top of my ear. A strand had sprouted there overnight and made me look like something out of *The Cat in the Hat*.

—*Bill Cosby*

I'm manic that I just turned thirty and my biological clock is tick, tick, ticking. Basically, I'm Ted Kaczynski with PMS. My boyfriend doesn't know it, but at any moment I could blow. During sex I dress up as a postal worker.

—*Tamara Kastle*

When you get older your body changes. Now I groan louder after a meal than I do after an orgasm.

—*Joel Warshaw*

When you're in your thirties it's very hard to make a new friend. Whatever group you've got now, that's who you're going with. You're not interviewing, you're not interested in seeing any applications. If I meet a guy at the gym or the club, it's like, "I'm sure you're a very nice person, you seem to have a lot of potential. We're just not hiring right now."

—Jerry Seinfeld

My friend Ann is in her thirties, single, and she's starting to feel that she has to choose between career and family. I say, don't put all your eggs in one basket. Use a cryogenic freezer instead.

—Lesley Wake

The older you get, you're just too tired to care about the same things. Rock concerts, I used to camp out for tickets. Now you could tell me Barbra Streisand is playing for free down the street, and I'd say, "How far down the street? Let's just stay here and watch the Discovery Channel. C'mon, it's Shark Week!"

—Kathleen Madigan

The telephone book of a middle-aged man is like Walt Disney's view of America: everyone forever living happily together. My address book has dozens of people I never will call again, especially the dead ones. My wife said, "The only name you don't have here is Booker T. Washington." "I'd better take care of that," I said. "I owe him a call."

—*Bill Cosby*

I'm officially middle-aged. I don't need drugs anymore, thank God. I can get the same effect just by standing up real fast.

—*Jonathan Katz*

My sister Kathryn has some crazy ideas about getting older. After forty years as a brunette, when her hair turned white, she decided that she'd become an albino. Yeah, Sis, and your wrinkles mean you're a shar-pei.

—*Daryl Hogue*

You know you're getting old when you get that one candle on the cake. It's like, "See if you can blow *this* out."

—*Jerry Seinfeld*

My uncle Max, he's ninety-four and still going strong. But sometimes he gets a little confused. He's marrying his third wife, and when I asked him, "Where's the honeymoon?" he said, "Viagra Falls."

—*Fran Chernowsky*

Airplanes

I hate flying in small planes. In the airport you see, "Flight 109: Departures, Arrivals—Odds."

—Billy Crystal

I finally understand why they let people with small children board first. Not because you need more time to put things away; they want to spare you all the dirty looks.

—Paul Reiser

Alcohol

Booze makes you loud. It's written on the label, "Alcohol percent by volume."

—Mark Lundholm

With my parents it was Alcoholics Unanimous. The first time I polished off a bottle of alcohol, it had a nipple on it. In my family, that was called baby-sitting.

—Atom

Jack Daniel's, that's a wild man drink. It should come with bail money. 'Cause on Jack you don't know where you're going to end up. But when you get there, you're not going to be wearing pants.

—Dave Attell

Anger

Women don't get mad at you about something you just did. They have precision memory, for *everything* you've ever done. Time, date, place, what you said, and your hand position when you said it. This memory will never crash. You bury her, and from six feet under you'll hear a muffled shout, *"At the church picnic, nineteen eighty-five. What kind of look was that you gave Kenesha, Mister Big Eyes!"*

—*Sinbad*

Animal Rights

My feeling is, we ran from animals for three million years, it's our time now. If a cow could eat you, it would. And it wouldn't care how comfortable your truck ride over was, either.

—*Greg Proops*

We get upset when dolphins get caught in tuna nets, but no one cares about the ten thousand dead tuna. Because they're not cute. Dolphins, on the other hand, have that great round, smiling face, the friendly eyes, the bald head. They look like your uncle Marvin. We can't slaughter anything that might show up for the holidays.

—*Paul Reiser*

I think animal testing is a terrible idea; they get nervous and give the wrong answers.

—*Fry and Laurie*

Animals

It's so weird all the different names they have for groups of animals. They have pride of lions, school of fish, rack of lamb . . .

— *Ellen DeGeneres*

My favorite animal is steak.

—*Fran Lebowitz*

We've all done this, because we're so mature. You see a cow on the side of the road, stick your head out the window, and go "Mooo!" Like we expect the cow to think, "Hey, there's another cow driving that car! How can he afford that?"

—*Garry Shandling*

In L.A. we get coyotes in our garbage cans. Coyotes are just like my relatives. They go out in pairs, they whine at night, and they go anywhere there's food.

—*Billy Crystal*

You know why fish are so thin? They eat fish.

—*Jerry Seinfeld*

Penguins mate for life. Which doesn't really surprise me, 'cause they all look exactly alike. It's not like they're gonna meet a better-looking penguin someday.

—*Ellen DeGeneres*

If you look at a platypus, you think that God might get stoned—"Okay, let's take a beaver and put on a duck's bill. It's a mammal, but it lays eggs. Hey, Darwin! Kiss my ass!"

—*Robin Williams*

Apartment

The only good thing about a singles' apartment is that you never had to clean it up. At least, not until the day you moved and tried to get your security deposit back. Then you'd argue with the landlord. "No sir, the back door was missing when we moved in here. The pizzas were always on the ceiling."

—*Jeff Foxworthy*

All of the people in my building are insane. The guy above me designs synthetic hairballs for ceramic cats. The lady across the hall tried to rob a department store with a pricing gun. She said, "Give me all of the money in the vault, or I'm marking down everything in the store."

—*Steven Wright*

Apocalypse

I always wanted to be the last guy on Earth, just to see if all those women were lying to me.

—*Ronnie Shakes*

Art

I'm taking an art class and the nude model just quit. Because I like to finger paint.

—*Wendy Liebman*

There is nothing funny about dogs playing poker. There is nothing remotely cute about animals with gambling problems. If you look closely at those paintings, you can tell that most of those dogs are playing with money they can't afford to lose. And sadder still, it takes seven of their dollars to make one of ours.

—*Dennis Miller*

When you look at some of Picasso's paintings, it makes you wonder what kind of women he visualized when he masturbated.

—*George Carlin*

Last year I went fishing with Salvador Dalí. He was using a dotted line. He caught every other fish.

—*Steven Wright*

Assembly Required

I got a gas grill, but it came unassembled. It looked like a car bomb. Every guy's been where I've been. You finish building it, it looks great, but there's a weird bag of important-looking stuff left over. "Honey? Why don't *you* try the grill out first? I'll be in the basement with my welding hat on."

—*Tim Allen*

Attitude

I'm sort of bitchy. But I like being bitchy. Because it means I don't have to deal with all those bothersome second dates.

—*Ann Oelschlager*

I'm paranoid. On my stationary bike I have a rear-view mirror.

—*Richard Lewis*

Baby

You have got to change those diapers every day. When it says six to twelve pounds on the side of the Pampers box, they're not lying. That is all those things will hold.

—*Jeff Foxworthy*

My friends have a baby. All you hear is, "You've got to come over and see the baby!" Nobody ever wants you to come over to see their grandfather. "He's so cute, a hundred and sixty-four pounds and four ounces. He's a thousand months. He went to the bathroom by himself today."

—*Jerry Seinfeld*

In some cultures they don't name their babies right away. They wait and see how the child develops, like in *Dances with Wolves*. Unfortunately, our kids' names would be less romantic and poetic. "This is my oldest boy, Falls Off His Tricycle, his friend Dribbles His Juice, and my beautiful daughter, Allergic to Nuts."

—*Paul Reiser*

I hate changing my baby's diapers after he poops. I know exactly what he ate at day care. Yesterday, it was carrots. Tomorrow I'm hoping for long-stemmed roses.

—*Shirley Lipner*

Shouldn't there be some kind of relationship between how much a baby eats and how much comes out the other end? It's like at the circus, where they've got the tiny VW Bug but the clowns just keep coming out and out and out. . . . Eventually you learn how to hold your breath like a Hokkaido pearl diver.

—*Dennis Miller*

My friend has a baby. I'm recording all the noises he makes, so later I can ask him what he meant.

—*Steven Wright*

The best thing is that baby intercom, so you can monitor your child. She's in her crib with her intercom, and can get me on mine, "Breaker One Nine, Dad. I've got spit-up on my shirt, and I'm packing a load. I could use some help out here."

—*Bob Saget*

From the jump, I was a high-tech daddy. I had this cool mountain backpack to carry my kids in. I was able to take them with me everywhere. The only drawback was, the babies pour that acidic Similac down your neck. But at least I have no more back hair.

—*Sinbad*

When you have a baby nobody ever checks to see if you're a good parent. When you adopt, they check. Those social services people drove me crazy. They called me every day, "You childproof the house yet? You childproof the house?" Yeah, he'll never get in here.

—*Margaret Smith*

I was sitting next to a young couple with a baby on the plane and I was making the baby laugh the entire flight. Do you know what babies love? Ethnic jokes.

—*Sarah Silverman*

Bald

You know you're going bald when your conversations with your barber keep getting shorter and shorter. I sit down. "How about those . . ." "Next." "What?" "We're done." "Well, here's a tip." "I can't. That would be stealing."

—*Dave Attell*

They say Al Gore is starting to lose his hair. I hope not. That's the only part of him that moves now.

—*Jay Leno*

I prefer balding men. Why would you want to run your hands through a man's hair when you could shove your fist right into his skull?

—*Stephanie Hodge*

I like being bald. I love walking around feeling that I'm getting away with being naked in public.

—*Atom*

Bar

Two guys walk into a bar. You'd think one of them would have seen it.

—*Daniel Lybra*

I was in a bar the other night, hopping from barstool to barstool, trying to get lucky. But there wasn't any gum under any of them.

—*Emo Philips*

I went to the bar to have a few drinks. The bartender asked me, "What'll you have?" I said, "Surprise me." He showed me a naked picture of my wife.

—*Rodney Dangerfield*

Bathing

I like to fill my tub up with water, then turn the shower on and act like I'm in a submarine that's been hit.

—*Steven Wright*

Bathroom

I live with a wonderful man. I lived with other men, too, and not one of them has had a clue what he was doing in the bathroom. I don't care how wonderful a man is, or isn't, surround his ass with tile and porcelain and his head explodes.

—*Whoopi Goldberg*

If there is a difference between men and women, it would have to be that men don't have to have a matching set for something to be functional. But a woman will not feel comfortable in a shower unless she approves of the shower curtain. "Just put the orange washcloth with the green towel, woman! They'll dry you all the same." She would rather stay funky than clash.

—*Sinbad*

Beach

During the summer I like to go to the beach and make sand castles out of cement. And wait for kids to run by and try to kick them over.

—*James Leemer*

Beauty Contest

They wanted to allow divorced women to compete in the Miss America pageant. Was that a good idea? Do you really want to hear, "My dreams for the future include world peace, and that my ex-husband gets killed by a bus"?

—*Jay Leno*

Bigotry

This man was a bigot and a bed wetter. He used to go to Ku Klux Klan meetings wearing a rubber sheet.

—*Woody Allen*

Birds

Eagles mate while flying at eighty miles an hour. And when they start to drop, they don't stop until the act is completed. So, it's not uncommon they both hit the ground, and die. Boy, don't we feel like wimps for stopping to answer the phone? I don't know about you, but if I'm one of those two birds and we're getting close to the ground, I would seriously consider faking it.

—*Ellen DeGeneres*

Birth

What they put women through today when they're having a baby! They don't want to medicate them, as compared to previous generations. When my mom had me, she had so much medication, she didn't wake up till I was seven.

—*Dennis Wolfberg*

My wife didn't want her drugs until after our daughter was born. I told her, "This is not the Olympics or a gladiator movie—when it hurts, take the damn Demerol!"

—*Tim Allen*

I used my Lamaze breathing when the anesthesiologist's bill came. But it sure didn't work when the real deal was going on. I was breathing in my wife's face, when she grabs me by the eyeball and shouts in my ear, "If you don't quit breathing that funky breath in my face, and get me some drugs quick, I am going to pull out this eye and throw it down the hall!"

—Sinbad

I was so ugly when I was born, the doctor slapped my mother.

—Henny Youngman

I was born by cesarean section, but you can't really tell. Except that when I leave my house, I always go out the window.

—Steven Wright

My friends want to show me films of their baby's birth. No, thank you. But I'll look at a video of the conception, if you've got one.

—Garry Shandling

Blood

I tried to give blood the other day. The blood bank refused to take it, though. Because I wouldn't tell them where I got it from.

—*Wally Wang*

Books

I'm writing a book. I've got the page numbers done.

—*Steven Wright*

Outside of a dog, a book is man's best friend. Inside a dog it's too dark to read.

—*Groucho Marx*

When you're a toddler, your favorite book isn't necessarily the one with the best story, or even the prettiest pictures. It's the one whose pages taste best. The book that goes easy on your gums is a great read. "I enjoy Faulkner's storytelling, but his novellas tend to cut me in the roof of the mouth. Dickens, on the other hand, soft and nice."

—*Paul Reiser*

You can't judge a book by its cover. I learned that teaching ninth-grade English. The *Hustler* is always hidden inside *Anne of Green Gables*.

—*Lesley Wake*

Bored

When I get real bored, I like to drive downtown and get a great parking spot. Then sit in my car and count how many people ask me if I'm leaving.

—*Steven Wright*

Bowling

I like to go to the bowling alley and bring a little black marble with me, and put it inside that machine that they use to polish the balls. Then call the manager over.

—*James Leemer*

Boyfriend

We were incompatible in a lot of ways. Like for example, I was a night person, and he didn't like me.

—*Wendy Liebman*

I'd like to have a boyfriend in prison, so I'd always know where he is.

—*Carrie Snow*

Boy Scout

They don't want gay kids in the Boy Scouts. But their motto is Be Prepared, and nobody's more prepared than a gay scout. My survival kit had a spice rack. My Swiss Army knife had a melon baller and garlic press. I was ready for anything.

—*Bob Smith*

Bra

I stuff my bra. So if you get to second base with me, you'll find that the bases are loaded.

—*Wendy Liebman*

My favorite marketing gimmick, the Wonderbra. Doesn't your date notice that your chest feels like a stuffed animal? And what happens when you take it off? It's called the Wonderbra because the guy is thinking, "I wonder where her boobs went?"

—*Rebecca Nell*

Breakup

I have an ex-boyfriend who wants to stay a friend. That means he wants to keep in touch and tell me how miserable I am without him. He wrote me a letter—"I'm now seeing someone smarter and more successful than you." I responded, "I'm now seeing someone older and balder than you." That'll show him.

—*Maura Kennedy*

The thing about breaking up when you get older, you just don't have the steam anymore. "Oh, that's it. I can't start shaving my legs above the knee again."

—*Elayne Boosler*

Breast Feeding

If I ever have a kid I'm definitely going to breast-feed it. Because I don't know how to cook. I would be breast-feeding him through college. His friends will be jealous.

—*Wendy Liebman*

That milk can flow from a breast is a miraculous miracle. But I can't get past the fact that food is coming out of my wife's breasts. What was once essentially an entertainment center has now become a juice bar.

—*Paul Reiser*

My mother never breast-fed me. She told me that she only liked me as a friend.

—*Rodney Dangerfield*

Breasts

In Los Angeles, you have to have breast implants. And an A-cup entitles you to park in a handicapped spot.

—*Jeannie Dietz*

I've got small boobs, and shopping for bras is torture. There's this new Water Bra, so you squish if someone hugs you. Mine had to be filled with so much water Sea World called. They're looking for a new habitat for Shamu.

—*Daryl Hogue*

Fake breasts, women always say, "You know they're not real, don't you? She bought them." I don't care if they're real. I want to buy some, too. For the house, put them in different rooms. And on the dashboard of the car, for when I'm driving.

—*Arsenio Hall*

Since I've been in remission for cancer, my four-year-old son has asked questions about my breast prosthesis. I put it in a box at night and take it out in the morning when I get dressed. For Share Day my son asked, "Mommy, can I take your breast in a box to school?" I said, "Yes, but be sure to return it. Daddy's going to need it tonight."

—*Liz Sells*

Brother

Older brothers invented terrorism. "Louie, see that swamp? There's a monster in it." So for years I walked way around it. Until I got a little older, a little wiser—and a little brother.

—*Louie Anderson*

My brother Clyde is a big old guy. When you open the dictionary to cool, Clyde's picture is there. Clyde has his own theme music. When he walks down the street or into a room, you can hear him coming.

—*Whoopi Goldberg*

Burial

A Jew dies, zoom, into the ground immediately. Gentiles have a wake, four days, eight shows a day, like vaudeville. Jews bury so quickly that old Jewish people are afraid to take a nap lest they be mistaken for dead.

—*Robert Klein*

Camping

I don't understand camping. Maybe it's because I'm from New York, where we call it homeless. I am not leaving my apartment to go lay outside.

—*Karen Williams*

A friend of mine says Jewish people don't camp. We do, we just have it catered. So I was camping up in the Sequoias, at the Sheraton . . .

—*Garry Shandling*

Camping. That's what I call getting drunk outside.

—*Dave Attell*

I hate camping. I don't see the fun in paying money to basically live like a homeless person. If I wanted to sleep in a tent for a night, it would be outside the mall the night before Nordstrom's half-yearly sale.

—*Stephanie Schiern*

I went camping and borrowed a circus tent by mistake. I didn't notice until I got it set up. People complained because they couldn't see the lake.

—*Steven Wright*

Cancer

I've been in remission from breast cancer for three years, and the hardest part was losing my breast. Now when I really want something, I can't say, "I'd give my left tit for that."

—*Liz Sells*

Coffee has carcinogens, causes cancer. And it also has caffeine. So not only are you dying, you watch yourself go.

—*Jackie Mason*

You show me something that doesn't cause cancer, and I'll show you something that isn't on the market yet.

—*George Carlin*

Scientists say they've found the way to turn normal cells into cancerous cells. Hello? That's called smoking.

—*Jay Leno*

Candy

My parents used to stuff me with candy when I was a kid. M&M's, jujubes, SweeTARTS. I don't think they wanted a child, I think they wanted a piñata.

—*Wendy Liebman*

Careers

Banker is swimming in the water. A shark comes toward him and veers away. Professional courtesy.

—*Henny Youngman*

When we were growing up my mother told my brother he was a pain in the neck. He became a chiropractor. I'm glad she didn't call him a pain in the ass.

—*Joel Warshaw*

The greatest pride, to this day, in a Jewish home is to have a son a doctor. Unless he's a little retarded . . . a lawyer. If his mind doesn't work at all . . . an accountant.

—*Jackie Mason*

My father wanted me to become a doctor, but I wanted to do something that required more imagination. So we compromised, and I became a hypochondriac.

—*Wally Wang*

A congressional hearing was held to address a nationwide shortage of firefighters. According to several employment experts, part of the problem is that many young people today are opting for better-paying jobs that don't involve such a high risk of catching on fire.

—*Craig Kilborn*

Realtors are people who did not make it as used-car salesmen.

—*Bob Newhart*

Shakespeare said, "Kill all the lawyers." That was before agents.

—*Robin Williams*

Cars

They recall a lot of cars. "We gotta get those cars back. We don't recall putting brakes in them."

—*Evan Davis*

Driving a convertible has changed my eating habits while driving. I used to eat those Hostess Mini Donut Gems with the white powdered sugar. Now at times I find I'm eating a bald donut with white junk on my face. "But, Officer, it was a donut!"

—*Paula Poundstone*

When you're a dad you can't keep your cool car. Fancy stereo, power windows, sunroof—the kids will kill all that stuff. Take an ordinary cookie. In the hands of a kid it becomes a sugar hand grenade. You take the car into the shop because chocolate chips are clogging the carburetor.

—*Sinbad*

Never lend your car to anyone to whom you've given birth.

—*Erma Bombeck*

I hate those new sport utility vehicles. I just got cut off by that new one, you know—the Ford Exhibitionist.

—*Daryl Hogue*

A friend of mine has a car phone and he has an answering machine for it. The message is, "Hi, I'm home right now, so I can't come to the phone. If you leave your name and number, I'll call you when I'm out."

—*Steven Wright*

Ford and Microsoft are getting together so you can buy a car on-line. However, note this. If you order a Ford over your computer and your computer crashes, the car will also explode.

—*Bill Maher*

I have a slow car that can't beat anything. If my car were a professional basketball team, it would be the Los Angeles Clippers.

—*Robert Murray*

I hate getting that smog check. Last week I bought a car, and it failed inspection. Which really sucks! Because the ozone layer is going, and soon we're going to need to breathe the smog my car can create.

—*Joel Warshaw*

They say that the car a man drives is an extension of his penis. Is that why so many men drive small, fast cars? You'd think they'd want to impress people by driving a 1968 Buick Le Sabre, missing a cylinder. Big and slow.

—*Jennifer Vally*

I tell ya, nothin' goes right. I bought a Japanese car. I turn on the radio. I don't understand a word they're sayin'.

—*Rodney Dangerfield*

My best friend got a truck. But she didn't want to be trendy, so she got a UPS truck. Laugh, but she can park it anywhere. Worldwide.

—*Wendy Liebman*

Catalogs

My wife and I got ourselves on every mailing list in the free world. All you have to do is buy one distinctly dumb product you don't need, and everyone with a catalog hears about it. "Hi! We understand you don't care what you spend money on anymore."

—*Paul Reiser*

Cats

I have cats because they have no artificially imposed, culturally prescribed sense of decorum. They live in the moment. If I had an aneurysm in the brain and dropped dead, I love knowing that, as the paramedics carry me out my cats are going to be swatting at that little toe tag.

—*Paul Provenza*

Cats are smarter than dogs. You can't get eight cats to pull a sled through snow.

—*Jeff Valdez*

Recently, a woman on an airplane shocked the other passengers when she breast-fed her cat in coach. True story. Now, I love my cat, she's diabetic and I inject her with insulin twice a day, but I would never breast-feed a cat. Unless, of course, my snuggle-buggles was really hungry-wungry.

—**Cathryn Michon**

If toast always lands butter-side down, and cats always land on their feet, what happens if you strap toast on the back of a cat and drop it?

—*Steven Wright*

The country of Jamaica has approved the growing of hemp for cat food. Experts say that if a cat spent its whole life eating hemp cat food, by the time it's five it'll have a street value of $22,000.

—*Jay Leno*

My cat Ethel is an indoor cat, but somehow she is sneaking out at night. Because the other morning I found a stamp on her paw. I wouldn't have noticed it myself, but I just bought this new black light and she passed right under it, and I said, "Hey, what's that on your paw?"

—*Ellen DeGeneres*

My cat has never been out of my apartment. Except when he goes to the vet, and they take his temperature rectally. So that's what he thinks the outside is. Which bothers me, because he sees me go out every day.

—*Jon Stewart*

One thing you can say about cats. They don't have to worry about kissing each other's asses—they can do that for themselves.

—*Dwight*

I once tried to commit suicide by jumping off a building. I changed my mind at the last minute, so I just flipped over and landed on my feet. Two little kittens nearby saw what happened and one turned to the other and said, "See, that's how it's done."

—*Steven Wright*

I had a cat once. That was the roughest night of sex I ever had.

—*Matt Vance*

Celebrities

The media is drawn to celebrities. We've even gotten to the point where we're interviewing models. What do we expect to learn from a model? "I put lipstick on my lips. I walk that way when they tell me. I go to the bathroom by myself."

—*Jim Gaffigan*

We should pass a new law: Nobody can get famous just by sleeping with a celebrity and getting naked in a magazine. You have to make a contribution to society first. You can still be in *Playboy,* you just have to do something worthwhile beforehand. "I developed a vaccine, and I'd like to show you my breasts." Go ahead, you've earned it.

—*Elayne Boosler*

Cindy Crawford said that she lost five pounds in the first three months of pregnancy because she got morning sickness. But, of course, when you're a supermodel with morning sickness, you're throwing up for two.

—*Jay Leno*

Doesn't Prince Charles look like somebody kissed a frog, and it didn't change all the way?

—*Wendy Liebman*

Essence magazine declared Puff Daddy their Man of the Year. Humble Puffy said, "Behind every great man is another great man's music to sample."

—*Chris Rock*

After a fact-finding trip to El Salvador, the National Labor Committee reported that the manufacturer of Kathie Lee Gifford's clothing line is still employing underage workers. Kathie Lee says those kids aren't making clothes, they're just contestants on her new quiz show, *Who Wants to Have Enough Money to Buy Rice?*

—*Craig Kilborn*

People are questioning whether Michael Jackson is really the father of his children. I'd say that the odds are about the same as the odds that Melissa Etheridge is the father of her child.

—*Mike Brennan*

That Mick Jagger, he could French-kiss a moose. He's got child-bearing lips.

—*Joan Rivers*

Ally McBeal, maybe it's time you tried an Ally McMeal.

—*David Spade*

E! was interviewing Kate Moss once and she said, "It's hard to be a model. Walking is hard, you've got to remember—right, left. And when you go down the runway, you have to turn around. I forgot to turn around one time, and I was lost for a week."

—*Le Maire*

I'm from Kentucky, a place with very few celebrities, but I did meet Colonel Sanders once. And my mom would always remind me, "Colonel Sanders is an icon of America!" Yeah, he's the Adolf Hitler of the chicken world. The man responsible for more animal deaths than every oil spill, baby seal hunt, and Ted Nugent barbecue combined.

—*Jim Wyatt*

Dr. Laura Schlessinger lost her court battle to prevent twenty-year-old nude pictures of her from being posted on the Internet. This is a terrible, terrible thing. Every time some celebrity is embarrassed by nude photos coming out, it makes it harder for us to get our girlfriends to pose naked.

—*Colin Quinn*

If O.J. wasn't famous he'd be in jail right now. If O.J. drove a bus, he wouldn't even be O.J. He'd be Orenthal, the Bus-driving Murderer.

—*Chris Rock*

Tori Spelling—is it just me, or does she have that tadpole-guppy thing going? Her eyes are on the side of the head. You have to stand to one side or the other to talk to her.

—*Le Maire*

When I found out that Steven Spielberg has two black kids, I was amazed. Where did he get those kids from? Were they props left over from *The Color Purple*?

—*Damon Wayans*

Steve Tyler of Aerosmith has such a set of teeth on him, when he goes to the dentist, the dentist says, "Nurse, get some Xrays of Mr. Tyler's mouth, when we get the Imax equipment."

—*Garry Shandling*

Cheating

My ex cheated, and came up with the worst lies in history. Four in the morning, she comes in with a champagne bottle, and when I ask, "Where were you?" she says, "I was seal hunting."

—*Richard Lewis*

Childhood

I'm an only child, and it wasn't always easy. A lot of games were hard to play. Like catch. God, that was tiring.

— *Dominic Dierkes*

My parents worked in the theater, so I was raised around show people. When I was three, they'd take me to a bar and make me stand on the table to sing show tunes. I was the only kid in preschool who asked for a Bud Light before I'd sing the alphabet song.

—*Thyra Lees-Smith*

I grew up the baby of eight kids, in a two-bedroom house. Ma never had to worry about curfew. You came home late, you didn't have any place to sleep. My brother was in bed five o'clock in the afternoon, eating dinner.

—*Mark Curry*

Once when I was lost I asked a policeman to help me find my parents. I asked him, "Do you think we'll ever find them?" He said, "I don't know, kid. There are so many places they can hide."

—*Rodney Dangerfield*

My childhood was pretty bad. When I was seven, my mother told me I was selfish when I asked for dinner. "You're just like your father," she said.

—*Gloria Brinkworth*

Your height and weight really determine how rough your childhood's going to be. On my first day of junior high school, some kids got robbed. But the guy turned me upside down and shook the money out of my pockets. That's what happens where you're little. A normal-sized guy would at least get the respect of being punched in the face before he got robbed.

—*Chris Rock*

When I was a child, I couldn't wait for the first snowfall. I would run to the door and yell, "Let me in! Let me in!" You know the deal.

—*Emo Philips*

Children

My mother loved children. She would have given anything if I had been one.

—*Groucho Marx*

Having children is like having a bowling alley in your brain.

—*Martin Mull*

I can't have children. Because I have white couches.

—*Carrie Snow*

I think about having children, because time is running out. I want to have children while my parents are still young enough to take care of them.

—*Rita Rudner*

In a nutshell, just be good and kind to your children, because not only are they the future of the world, they are the ones who can eventually sign you into the home.

—*Dennis Miller*

Clichés

If you can't beat them, arrange to have them beaten.

—*George Carlin*

If it ain't broke, you can probably still fix it. That's my motto.

—*Tim Allen*

I hate people who, no matter what happens, have something positive to say. Yesterday I overheard someone say, "Every cloud has a silver lining." To hell with that, show me the cloud with the hard cash.

—*Joel Warshaw*

Curiosity killed the cat. But for a while I was a suspect.

—*Steven Wright*

I think the expression "It's a small world" is really a euphemism for "I keep running into people I can't stand."

—*Brock Cohen*

Benjamin Franklin was wrong. In my experience, "Early to bed, and early to rise" makes a man dull, anal, and horny.

—*Gloria Brinkworth*

The early bird gets the worm. I'd rather sleep in and have toaster muffins.

—*Shirley Lipner*

The lion and the calf shall lie down together, but the calf won't get much sleep.

—*Woody Allen*

They say that blondes have more fun. Blondes don't have more fun, people just expect so little from them, they have all the free time in the world.

—*Stephanie Hodge*

If truth is beauty, how come no one has their hair done in a library?

—*Lily Tomlin*

A watched pot never boils. But it does get paranoid.

—*Lesley Wake*

It's an ill wind that blows when you leave the hairdresser.

—*Phyllis Diller*

A word to the wise ain't necessary. It's the stupid ones who need the advice.

—*Bill Cosby*

You can get more with a kind word and a gun than you can with a kind word alone.

—*Johnny Carson*

I hate clichés. They're such a bunch of hooey. Don't bite the hand that feeds you? Yeah, shoot it and keep all the food for yourself.

—Ann Oelschlager

They say, "Today is the first day of the rest of your life." No, yesterday was. Today is the second day, when I realized it wasn't such a good idea to eat at Denny's after all.

—Jared Krichevsky

Clothing

When you're a kid, your mother's job is to make you look like a dork. The mittens pinned to your jacket, the Elmer Fudd earflap hat, the rubber boots with the Wonder bread bags over your feet. And, of course, the pièce de résistance, the snow pants. There's an outfit that screams, "Beat the shit out of me, and take my lunch money!"

—Dennis Miller

Exercise fosters unhealthy ideas about small, clingy shirts and low-slung jeans. Constricting clothing limits oxygen flow to the brain, thereby reducing personality capacity among the physically fit. The sins of pride are usually located near the StairMaster. So stay pure, and sit down.

—Janeane Garofalo

I'm reading "Hints from Heloise," and she says that if you put an angora sweater in the freezer for an hour, it won't shed for the rest of the day. And I'm thinking, "My cat sheds an awful lot."

—*Ellen DeGeneres*

For men, upon marriage you lose the ability to choose clothing for yourself. "Honey, what do you think? A striped shirt and a solid tie, or a solid shirt and a pair of mukluks? A Beatle wig and a grass skirt? Tell me, because I haven't used that part of my brain in several years. Why don't you just choose something, lay it out, and I'll be in the crib until we have to leave."

—*Paul Reiser*

I have two different colored socks on. But to me they're the same, because I go by thickness.

—*Steven Wright*

I was out of clean underwear. I had to dig through the drawer for that Undie of Last Resort. Some briefs from the Ming dynasty, with a safety pin. Finally I get all desperate, got a tube sock, some duct tape—I'm a panty McGyver. Can't find panties, I will make my own.

—*Aisha Tyler*

You ever wear a bathing suit 'cause you've run out of clean underwear?

—*Louis C. K.*

College

I went to college, I graduated. I majored in alcoholism, with a minor in communications. Which now qualifies me to speak drunk in public.

—*Joel Warshaw*

I had a dual major in college, engineering and English. But I never completed the liberal arts degree, because I already knew how to get a minimum wage job by myself.

—*Wally Wang*

When kids go to college now, they bring personal computers. When I went to college, everyone brought a personal bong. And if you didn't have one, you could always sign up for time at the University Bong Center.

—*Norman K.*

I think football is an important part of college life. At some schools, it's the only chance the team gets to see the campus.

—*Gene Perret*

My parents sent my brother through law school. He graduated. Now he's suing them for wasting seven years of his life.

—*Mike Binder*

Comedy

Comedy is when you accidentally fall off a cliff and die. Tragedy is when I have a hangnail.

—*Mel Brooks*

There's no trick to being a humorist when you have the whole government working for you.

—*Will Rogers*

People always ask me, "Were you funny as a child?" No, I was an accountant.

—*Ellen DeGeneres*

When I told my friends I was going to be a comedian, they laughed at me.

—*Carrot Top*

Communication

Only a man will think of a burp as a greeting for another man.

—*Tim Allen*

The two most beautiful words in the English language are "check enclosed."

—*Dorothy Parker*

I personally think we developed language because of our deep inner need to complain.

—*Lily Tomlin*

Comparisons

I'm shopping, and I caught this guy who's comparing apples and oranges. So I walked over and said, "Hey, you can't do that." He said, "Why not?" "Because it would be like . . . forget it."

—*James Leemer*

Computers

As anyone who has ever tried to purchase a PC knows, computer technology moves faster than Luciano Pavarotti going after a Cinnabun. No matter which computer you buy, no matter how much you spend, by the time you get it to your car—it's an eight-track tape player.

—*Dennis Miller*

I got a computer. I wrote an apology note to my VCR for ever thinking it was difficult. You find someone in this country who can print out an envelope. Maybe the fifth envelope, but you have to kill four to get to the fifth one.

—*Elayne Boosler*

They say that computers can't think, but I have one that does. It thinks it's broken.

—*Gene Perret*

IBM is spending ten million dollars to develop a computer that thinks like a person. They've already made a computer think like one of the Spice Girls, but that's because they forgot to plug it in.

—*Wally Wang*

Condom

The new medical crisis. Doctors are reporting that many men are having allergic reactions to latex condoms. They say they cause severe swelling. So what's the problem?

—*Jay Leno*

I don't understand why some guys get self-conscious when they buy condoms. I don't get embarrassed when I buy condoms; I get embarrassed when I throw them out after they expire.

—*Jack Archey*

Contraception

The most effective birth control I know is a toddler with the croup and diaper rash.

—*Kate Zannoni*

Cooking

I used to be very creative, I could make a complete gourmet dinner using only two cans. I had to stop, though. The sanitation guys took away the cans.

—*Fran Chernowsky*

I'm a good cook. I can make fruit!

—*Tanya Luckerath*

The Great Chefs of Ireland, that would be a thick book, wouldn't it? It would be a pamphlet saying, "Try another country."

—*Tim Allen*

I made lobster recently. I'm squeamish, I didn't want to kill it. So I just boiled the water and played some Michael Bolton tapes. It committed suicide.

—*Wendy Liebman*

Cosmetics

Makeup is such a weird concept. I wake up in the morning, and look in the mirror: "Gee, I really don't look so good. Maybe if my eyelids were blue, I'd be more attractive."

—*Cathy Ladman*

In high school I had the worst case of acne ever. And my mother told me boys didn't ask me out because I didn't wear enough makeup. Hello! If you can't see enough of these revolting scars and bumps, let me highlight them with Rosebud Spring from Revlon! That's like putting spotlights on landfill to lure prospective home buyers.

—*Ann Oelschlager*

I don't wear makeup because I was raised by the wolves. All male wolves. They didn't wear makeup. Although one did wear deodorant, so I learned about that. So that's good.

—*Ellen DeGeneres*

I wear so much makeup you could stick a finger on my face and write "Wash Me." I know my makeup looks good when I can put a dipstick in it and get a reading.

—*Le Maire*

I put on fake nails once, those surfboard Satan nails from hell. But I couldn't do anything, they're useless! The only thing they're good for is starting an orange. Or while you're choking . . . tracheotomy!

—*Sue Murphy*

Where lipstick is concerned, the important thing is not color but to accept God's final word on where your lips end.

—*Jerry Seinfeld*

Don't fiddle with women's stuff when they're not around. "What happened to my eyeliner pencil?" "Ohhhh. The phone rang, I couldn't find anything else to write with. It's just a pencil, I'll go replace it." Thirty-eight bucks, and a decent command of the French language later . . .

—*Tim Allen*

Court

The judge asked, "What do you plead?" I said, "Insanity, Your Honor. Who in their right mind would park in the passing lane?"

—*Steven Wright*

Credit Card

I hate when they call up to check if your credit card is good. I always feel like they're talking about me. "You won't believe what he's buying now!"

—*Jerry Seinfeld*

Crime

A seventeen-year-old Amish boy was arrested outside Cleveland for driving his horse and buggy while under the influence of alcohol. Police said they suspected he was drunk when they witnessed him stop at a filling station and stick a gasoline nozzle in his horse's ass. If convicted, the boy could face twenty-five years of hard labor. However, if found innocent, he could face twenty-five years of hard labor.

—*Craig Kilborn*

The Bank of New York is in trouble because they were laundering money from the Russian mob. They ran as much as ten billion dollars through a single account. And they still didn't qualify for the free checking.

—*Bill Maher*

I have no respect for gangs today. None. They just drive by and shoot people. At least in the old days, like in *West Side Story,* the gangs used to dance with each other first.

—*Robert G. Lee*

It's a shame so many people are killing each other these days. It used to be if you wanted to shoot at a total stranger, you had to wait until deer hunting season.

—*Wally Wang*

An escaped murderer who had been loose three weeks recently gave himself up. He couldn't cope with the modern conveniences of life that weren't around when he went to jail twenty years ago. He couldn't deal with the ATMs, he couldn't get gas from a self-service pump, and when he went into the Gap, all the clothes looked like his prison uniform.

—*Bill Maher*

O. J. Simpson was the victim of an attempted robbery. When the police asked him what kind of gun the assailant had, O.J. said, "Don't ask me, I'm a knife man."

—*Jay Leno*

Ninety-eight percent of the adults in this country are decent, hardworking, honest Americans. It's the other two percent that get all the publicity. But then, we elected them.

—*Lily Tomlin*

In Germany, police are searching for a woman who holds men at gunpoint and forces them to have sex with her. Actually the gun isn't for the sex, it's to keep the guy around later to make him cuddle.

—*Jay Leno*

What the hell is wrong with these white kids shooting up the schools? Soon you're gonna have little white kids saying, "I want to go to a black school, where it's *safe*."

—*Chris Rock*

The crime problem in New York is getting really serious. The other day the Statue of Liberty had both hands up.

—*Jay Leno*

Cruise

My wife and I went on a three-day cruise. Actually, it was more like a three-day meal. They tell you to bring just one out-fit, but in three different sizes: large, extra-large, and blimp.

—*Robert G. Lee*

Dance

My friend would spend all of his time practicing limbo. He got pretty good. He could go under a rug.

—*Steven Wright*

Dating

Why do we fix people up? You thought they'd have a good time, and it's a little power trip for you, isn't it? Now you're playing God. And of course, he was the first to fix people up, God fixed up Adam and Eve. "She's nice. She's very free about her body, doesn't wear much. She was going out with a snake, but I think that's over."

—*Jerry Seinfeld*

If you got fixed up on a blind date by your very best friend, wouldn't you think that within the top ten descriptive adjectives, lazy eye would be mentioned? We went out for a while, but I found out he was seeing someone on the side.

—*Caroline Rhea*

I like to date short guys, because we women love anything we can throw into our purse. "Let's see, keys, lipstick—oh, I forgot I was dating you, and you've eaten all my Altoids."

—*Le Maire*

Dating is a lot like sports. You have to practice, you work out, you study the greats. You hope to make the team, and it hurts to be cut.

—*Sinbad*

Let's begin by discussing dinner dates. This concept of traditional courting bothers me. I don't want food interrupting my two grueling days of predate starvation.

—*Janeane Garofalo*

My favorite thing to do on a date is go to dinner. Or should I say, have somebody else pay for my food.

—*Rebecca Nell*

An average guy makes a date with a girl. It costs him one hundred dollars, two hundred dollars. I make a date with a girl, it costs me nothing. I come up to her house, she wants to go out—I let her go! What's my business? I have to follow her around?

—*Jackie Mason*

I don't get no respect. A girl phoned me and said, "Come on over, there's nobody home." I went over. Nobody was home.

—*Rodney Dangerfield*

A man on a date wonders if he'll get lucky. The woman knows.

—*Monica Piper*

I was going out with this guy who was thirty and living at home with his parents. Course he's one of these guys who has to say these loud things during sex. It was the ugliest thing ever when he started shouting, "Mommy, Mommy! Mommy, Mommy!" So his mother comes running in. And I'm there naked, and he's crying, and all I can think to say is, "He started it!"

—Laura Kightlinger

When you're young, you think, "I'll never date a chick who has a kid. If she has a kid, I don't want her." You get a little older, you go, "I'll never go out with a chick who has two kids." You get a little older, you go, "Hey, man, her kids are well-behaved!"

—Willie Barcena

Younger guys have been approaching me lately. And asking me to buy them alcohol.

—Wendy Liebman

It's hard to meet someone new. But it's easy for this friend of mine, because she has very low standards. Like, she'll go home with a guy just for the free T-shirt.

—Jann Karam

Instead of going to bars, I just download my favorite cyber-guy, and click on User Support.

—*Sue Bova*

I'm dating a guy now, he's on TV. You might know him, he's on *America's Most Wanted.* He looks better than that sketch. But I'm telling your right now, whenever he gets out of line, I go, "Hey, I've got the 1-800 number, buddy."

—*Rosie O'Donnell*

I'm back-dating my target group to older men. My girl-friends are always asking about my dates, "Is he cute?" I'll just settle for a healthy prostate.

—*Maura Kennedy*

I'm dating the Pope. But I'm just using him to get to God.

—*Judy Tenuta*

I'm dating again, but it's got me confused. So I've been reading up on the differences between men and women. I read *The Rules,* the Mars and Venus books, *Dating for Dummies.* And here's the real difference—women buy the books.

—*Daryl Hogue*

Daughter

My daughter looks just like the cable man. But we get free HBO, so to hell with it.

—*Bob Saget*

I have adapted the philosophy of Genghis Khan, "Give a man a fish, and he eats for a day; teach a man to fish and he eats for a lifetime," for my slogan: "Show a teenage boy a gun, and he'll have your daughter home before 11:30 P.M."

—*Sinbad*

Death

Death should not be seen as the end, but as a very effective way to cut down expenses.

—*Woody Allen*

When I die, I'm going to leave my body to science fiction.

—*Steven Wright*

I tell ya, I get no respect from anyone. I bought a cemetery plot. The guy said, "There goes the neighborhood!"

—*Rodney Dangerfield*

They say such nice things about people at their funerals that it makes me sad to realize I'm going to miss mine by just a few days.

—*Garrison Keillor*

Even very young children need to be informed about dying. Explain the concept of death very carefully to your child. This will make threatening him with it much more effective.

—*P. J. O'Rourke*

For three days after death, hair and fingernails continue to grow, but phone calls taper off.

—*Johnny Carson*

I know when I'm going to die. My birth certificate has an expiration date on it.

—*Steven Wright*

The chief problem about death, incidentally, is the fear that there may be no afterlife. A depressing thought, particularly for those who have bothered to shave.

—*Woody Allen*

Dentist

I have the biggest crush on my dentist. He's so cute, I've been gargling with Coke. But it's hard to flirt with your dentist. "You have a cavity." "I know, and I'd like you to fill it."

—*Caroline Rhea*

I lost my front tooth, and my insurance company wouldn't cover its replacement, claiming it was for "cosmetic purposes." So what's a root canal—an entertainment expense?

—*Stephanie Schiern*

I don't get no respect. I told my dentist my teeth are going yellow. He told me to wear a brown necktie.

—*Rodney Dangerfield*

Diet

Nobody diets anymore, it's all exercise. Remember when we dieted in the eighties? The diet that I liked was the Fresca, M&M's, and cocaine diet. That was a great diet, but you can't do that anymore. You can't find Fresca.

—*Corey Kahane*

Never let your caloric intake exceed your white blood cell count.

—*Beth Donahue*

I've been on every diet in the world. I've been on Slim-Fast, yeah. For breakfast you have a shake. For lunch, you have a shake. For dinner you kill anyone with food on their plate.

—*Rosie O'Donnell*

The second day of a diet is always easier than the first. By the second you're off it.

—*Jackie Gleason*

Discrimination

White people don't know how to tell the difference between one black man and another. To white people, Ed Bradley and Bryant Gumbel waiting to cross the street together is scary. Clarence Thomas in an Adidas warm-up suit will not get a cab in Washington, D.C.

—*Chris Rock*

Divorce

Isn't a divorce when you pay a lawyer a lot of money to arrange it so you can move out, and leave everything you own with someone you hate? On the other hand, we can also regard divorce as the legal alternative to murder. In most cases.

—*Jeff Foxworthy*

It should be easy. You should be able to move on, with a letter of resignation. If you can write your own stupid wedding vows, why can't you write yourself out of the marriage? If bad poetry can get you married, bad poetry should be able to spring you. "You were my sunshine/Now you're my rain/Turned out you were nothin'/But a bad butt pain!"

—*Sinbad*

It's tough. After five years of marriage, it's difficult to lose the one with the good credit rating.

—*Rich Voss*

When it comes to divorce, absence may not make the heart grow fonder, but it sure cuts down on the gunplay.

—*Eileen Courtney*

My parents celebrated their forty-third wedding anniversary, so my mother don't want to hear me talking about divorce. "You gotta learn how to work these things out. Your father and I had a shoot-out, he took one in the arm. He was wrong, I shot him. You move on."

—*Wanda Sykes-Hall*

I'm a divorced, single mother. That's like God saying to you, "Thank you for playing the Marriage Game. Sorry you didn't win, but we have this lovely parting gift for you."

—*Corey Kahane*

When I was a teenager, I asked my mother, "Mom, are you and Dad getting a divorce?" "No, I'm just drying your father's clothes." But Dad was still in them.

—*Robert Murray*

I try too hard to be politically correct. Whenever I fill out an application for a credit card, under marital status, I write "pre-owned."

—*Fran Chernowsky*

Doctor

It takes so damn long to see a doctor, I think my HMO's trying to kill me. I called to get a strange mole checked out, but the first available appointment was six months. I said, "By then I could be dead." And the receptionist replied, "If that happens, be sure to cancel your appointment."

—*Stephanie Schiern*

I hate the waiting room, so sometimes I start screwing around with the stuff. Take all the tongue depressors out, lick them, put them back. Two can play at this waiting game.

— *Jerry Seinfeld*

All doctors are crooks. Why do you think when a doctor writes out a prescription, only he and the druggist can read it? Because they all say the same thing, "I got my money, you get yours."

—*Jackie Mason*

I've got a wonderful doctor. If you can't afford the operation, he touches up the X rays.

—*Henny Youngman*

Dogs

My husband and I are either going to buy a dog or have a child. We can't decide whether to ruin our carpet or ruin our lives.

—*Rita Rudner*

I once had a dog who really believed he was man's best friend. He kept borrowing money from me.

—*Gene Perret*

Dogs hate it when you blow in their face. I'll tell you who really hates that, my grandmother. Which is odd, because when we're driving she loves to hang her head out the window.

—*Ellen DeGeneres*

Some scientist spent twenty years in the lab inventing ice cream for dogs. He made it taste like vanilla, so it's hardly selling at all. If he'd made it taste like doody, dogs would be robbing stores with guns.

—*Elayne Boosler*

My parents' dog is an idiot. When I swim in their pool, Brandy runs along the edge, barking at me. Mom says, "She thinks you're drowning. She's just like Lassie." No, Lassie would jump in and try to save me. If I fell down a well Brandy would sit on the edge and wonder, "Any cookies down there?"

—*Stephanie Schiern*

I tell ya, my dog is lazy. He don't chase cars. He sits on the curb and takes down license plate numbers.

—*Rodney Dangerfield*

Last year for my birthday I was given a puppy. It's half poodle, and half pit bull. Not a good attack dog, but a vicious gossip.

—*Bob Smith*

It's always the little dogs you see wearing sweaters. My neighbor's dog has a sweater, but he wears it just wrapped around his shoulders.

—*Ellen DeGeneres*

Forget watchdogs. We have two big, friendly dogs. And Senta, who weighs in at 130 pounds, is also deathly afraid of . . . balloons. So we're really in trouble if a clown ever breaks in.

—*Daryl Hogue*

My mother gave my grandmother a Yorkshire terrier with this affliction, it shakes and shakes. Maybe someone told him to shake once and didn't say when to stop. He's like a shoe buffer. You can put your foot down there, and your shoe comes out shiny.

—*Garry Shandling*

Drinking

To teach kids about drinking, many schools now sponsor alcohol awareness programs. Don't we have something like that already? I believe they're called colleges.

—*Wally Wang*

I drink too much. Last time I gave a urine sample there was an olive in it.

—*Rodney Dangerfield*

Ever black out? You're drinking, you black out. You wake up in another bar. You're drinking, you black out. You wake up playing that knife game with an Indian, somewhere in South Dakota. You're drinking, you black out. You wake up, you're in White Castle, working three years, still not assistant manager.

—*Dave Attell*

My dad was the town drunk. A lot of times that's not so bad, but New York City?

—*Henny Youngman*

The American Medical Association announced that a drink a day is good for you. And I'm proud to announce that my father has covered my family for the next thirty-six generations. Some people are covered by Blue Cross, we're covered by Pabst Blue Ribbon.

—*Greg Fitzsimmons*

Driving

I am the worst driver. Let's just say I always wear clean underwear. I should drive a hearse and cut out the middleman.

—*Wendy Liebman*

Dads never want anyone else to drive. Mine especially. On his way out the door, he'd announce, "I'll do the goddamn driving. I was in a war!"

—*Louie Anderson*

Driving on the freeway is like hand-washing my delicate clothes. It's a big hassle, it takes longer than I expect, and I end up with my panties in a wad.

—*Lesley Wake*

The problem with the designated driver program is it's not a desirable job. But if you ever get suckered into doing it, have fun with it. At the end of the night, drop them off at the wrong house.

—*Jeff Foxworthy*

I hate freeway jockeys. They whip in and out of traffic at ninety miles per hour, trying to kill themselves and everyone else in their path, mad because God gave them a teeny-weeny toolbox to play with. So I shorten their misery by yelling out the window, "Get an implant! And leave the driving to us."

—*Gloria Brinkworth*

I've become so vain. I went through one of those traffic lights that take a picture when you go through a red light. I hated the picture, so I went through the light again. By the third time, I was pretty confident in front of the camera.

—*Le Maire*

I have my learner's permit, which means that I can drive with my parents in the car. Woohoo, I'm living on the edge. But driving with my parents isn't the wild ride you would think, oh no. It's actually very awkward, especially on dates. Because we're in the car at a drive-in, things start getting a little hot in the backseat, and finally I just have to turn around and say, "Mom, Dad—will you cut it out! We're trying to watch the movie up here!"

—*Dominic Dierkes*

Whenever I pick up a hitchhiker I say, "Put your seat belt on, I want to try something I saw in a cartoon."

—*Steven Wright*

I'm from Milwaukee, the only city in America where they put your bowling average on your driver's license. A cop will pull you over and ask how fast you were going, until he sees your license. "Two twenty-six? Hey, be more careful next time."

—*Dobie Maxwell*

Being on a Los Angeles freeway is a lot like being in a bar. It's a great place to be if you want to run into a drunk.

—*Robert Murray*

Mopeds. It's like you're on a hair dryer. Dogs are walking faster than you're going.

—*Eddie Izzard*

The difference between L.A. and New York drivers is that L.A. drivers tend to swerve all over the highway. New York drivers rarely have this problem. The body in the trunk makes a great stabilizer.

—*Brock Cohen*

I had to stop driving my car for a while. The tires got dizzy.

—*Steven Wright*

When you're stuck in traffic, you hate everybody. "Oh, look at this idiot. Why doesn't he just *Go*? Come on, go go go go GO! If you would just go, there wouldn't be traffic. That's why there's traffic; your failure to go!"

—*Paul Reiser*

My big fear: driving behind a truck with those big iron rebars. Truck stops, the bar goes right through my forehead. It doesn't kill me, they can't remove it—and I have to accessorize it.

—*Carrie Snow*

I'll put out my cigarette the day people walk in Hollywood. Where there is not one iota of unpaved space, and yet everyone feels the need to drive a suburban four-wheel Humvee assault vehicle. Because you never know when you're going off-road. "Kids, we're going through the drive-thru! Hold the roll bar, stay low!"

—*Greg Proops*

Drugs

I'm not into drugs. Maybe it's because doing drugs is often about sharing things, like joints and cocaine. I'm an only child, I don't share.

—*Joy Behar*

I don't do drugs, because I saw what it did to my friends. I'd get stoned, and they'd look really weird to me.

—*Wendy Liebman*

Stay away from cocaine. Oh, it might seem glamorous at first. But one day, one day, it will be your turn to buy.

—*Emo Philips*

I used to do drugs. I still do drugs. But I used to, too.

—*Mitch Hedberg*

I would never advocate the use of dope. Because I'm not a professional athlete, and I can't get my hands on the good stuff.

—*Greg Proops*

In high school, I could not pass a math test. I couldn't pass a drug test either. There may be a correlation there.

— *Lynda Montgomery*

Pat Buchanan's scandals are a little different than other politicians' scandals. For example, he experimented with drugs, he said—but only on prisoners.

—*Bill Maher*

The 1960s were when hallucinogenic drugs were really, really big. And I don't think it's a coincidence that we had the shows then like *The Flying Nun*.

—*Ellen DeGeneres*

I don't smoke marijuana any more. I don't smoke it any less either. I think it leads to harder stuff, like Ben & Jerry's ice cream and Snickers candy bars.

—*Jerry Rubin*

I think it's supersad when people are too old and addicted to pot. I was at a party and this guy with a gray, greasy ponytail and a bald spot comes up to me and says, "Hey, man, I got a new roach clip!" It's so pathetic, I want to say, "Grow up. Be an alcoholic!"

—Cathryn Michon

The marijuana report commissioned by the drug czar Barry McCaffrey came out. And it says that marijuana is very useful in treating pain, nausea, and weight loss. The downside is, it makes Andy Rooney seem funny.

—Bill Maher

This country has declared war on drugs to help protect the economy. Because if too many people get addicted to crack, there won't be enough of us left to be hooked on cigarettes and alcohol.

—Wally Wang

According to a new survey 60 percent of adults say they're aware of someone who's gone to work under the influence of drugs. Apparently the other 40 percent have never heard of the Dallas Cowboys.

—Conan O'Brien

A recent government study reported that 8 percent of full-time employees are on drugs at work. I think this study is flawed. The figure is too low. Because that 8 percent are only the people so stoned they answered yes to the question.

—*Bill Maher*

Earthquake

For those of you easterners, an earthquake may not be easy to visualize. Have you ever seen a range of mountains doing the Funky Chicken? My zip code changed three times and I was still in bed.

—*Bob Hope*

I know if I was in a big earthquake, I'd be the dude trapped in his car under a bridge. My luck, I'd have my radio dial stuck on the easy listening station. "Cut faster, here comes a block of ABBA!"

—*Tom Rhodes*

I'm not keeping canned goods in my apartment for an earthquake. If I get trapped beneath a beam for three days, at least I'll lose some weight.

—*Paula Poundstone*

Eating Disorders

Anorexia is just another word for nothing left to lose.

—*Joy Behar*

I have the opposite of anorexia, I think I'm thin. I'm in a support group. We all sit around in skin-tight clothing going, "Is this too baggy to wear?"

—*Caroline Rhea*

You've got bad eating habits if you use a grocery cart in the 7-Eleven, okay?

—*Dennis Miller*

Electricity

I used to live in a house that ran on static electricity. If you wanted to run the blender, you had to rub balloons on your head. If you wanted to cook, you had to pull off a sweater real quick.

—*Steven Wright*

Electricity can be dangerous. My nephew tried to stick a penny into a plug. Whoever said a penny doesn't go far didn't see him shoot across that floor. I told him he was grounded.

—*Tim Allen*

Embarrassment

You ever go to a big party, go in the bathroom, flush the toilet, and the water starts coming up? This is the most frightening moment in the life of a human being.

—*Jerry Seinfeld*

Emergency

I filled out an application that said, "In case of emergency notify . . ." I wrote, "Doctor." What's my mother going to do?

—*Steven Wright*

Engagement

You ever notice the word *engaged* has the word *gag* in the middle of it? Just something to think about, ladies.

—*Rosie O'Donnell*

Environmental Issues

In New York we have medical waste wash up onshore. Twenty years ago I had my appendix removed; I found it at Jones Beach. Thank God I didn't have a sex change.

—*Danny McWilliams*

New images from NASA show that the hole in the ozone is once again emerging over Antarctica. The South Pole

Tourist Bureau says it hopes to capitalize on this latest news by changing its slogan from "Antarctica: Frozen Hellhole" to the new, catchier "Antarctica: Gateway to Melanoma."

—*Craig Kilborn*

Ethnic

My father is from Ireland, and he's got a thick brogue. When I was a kid my friends would make fun of him, but he never knew it. They'd call, and when he'd answer the phone they'd say, "Rosie was after me Lucky Charms. The frosted-oat cereal with sweet surprises." He'd write it all down. "Jackie said, 'Manly, yes. But I like it, too!'"

—*Rosie O'Donnell*

I'm French, and I agree with you, the French are rude. But they know how to kiss. If it wasn't for the French, you would still wonder, "What the hell am I supposed to do with my tongue?"

—*Jim Rez*

You know who make the best boyfriends? Latin men. But, oh my goodness, I had no idea that Latin men were so noisy in bed. I didn't even know that there were that many saints.

—*Caroline Rhea*

Boy, those French. They have a different word for everything.

—*Steve Martin*

I married a German. Every night I dress up as Poland and he invades me.

—*Bette Midler*

Exercise

Homo sapiens did not labor to walk upright, only to damage their spines in step class.

—*Janeane Garofalo*

The word *aerobics* comes from two Greek words: *aero,* meaning "ability to," and *bics,* meaning "withstand tremendous boredom."

—*Dave Barry*

My doctor told me to exercise. He said walking would get me into shape. I said, "Doc, I've already chosen a shape, and it's round."

—*Irv Gilman*

I ran three miles today. Finally I said, "Lady, take your purse!"

—*Emo Philips*

I'm so tired of exercising. I think five thousand sit-ups should be pretty much permanent. You should be at home, you're on your last and final jumping jack, and you get that phone call, "Congratulations! You have completed the exercise portion of your life. Welcome to the incessant eating section."

—*Jann Karam*

I'm not working out. My philosophy: No pain, no pain.

—*Carol Leifer*

My wife and I start each morning with the genuine intention of exercising. But in a dazzling display of mutual support, we've learned to talk ourselves right out of it. "I don't feel like working out, you don't feel like working out. Let's just skip it." "We'll just look the way we do. And if anybody asks—we ran."

—*Paul Reiser*

I go running when I have to. When the ice cream truck is doing sixty.

—*Wendy Liebman*

I get my exercise at the supermarket. First I try to wrestle the plastic bags open. Then I give up, and roll my fruits and vegetables down the conveyor belt one at a time. It's my kind of bowling.

—*Fran Chernowsky*

A new study says that one of the advantages of the treadmill is that it's the highest calorie burner of the exercises. And the other advantage is that hamsters can now laugh at us.

—*Johnny Robish*

I like long walks. Especially when they are taken by people who annoy me.

—*Fred Allen*

I tried yoga because I heard you get to do your exercise laying down, so I signed right up for that.

—*Corey Kahane*

I took an aggression training course. The Basic Bitch Workout. I'm certified. I give new meaning to that time of the month. I no longer just get cramps; now I can give them.

—*S. Rachel Lovey*

Family

Your family is a pack of idiots you have to love. We exist on earth to love each other, and our family is the test.

—*Jeff Foxworthy*

Blood may be thicker than water, but it is still sticky, unpleasant, and generally nauseating.

—*Janeane Garofalo*

I went home for the holidays, and all the men in my family are bald, and all the women are fat. It's like a Metallica concert going on in my own home.

—*Dave Attell*

In my family, where back-biting and rejection run rampant, having a happy childhood was as likely as Jeffrey Dahmer being the food critic for the *New York Times*.

—*Gloria Brinkworth*

When I was young I used to think my people didn't like me. Because they used to send me to the store for bread, and then they'd move.

—*Richard Pryor*

Happiness is having a large, loving, caring, close-knit family in another city.

—*George Burns*

I looked up my family tree and found out I was the sap.

—*Rodney Dangerfield*

I'm a godmother. That's a great thing, to be a godmother. She calls me God for short; that's cute. I taught her that.

—*Ellen DeGeneres*

My mother is Mormon and my father is Moslem. I've got polygamy on both sides. My mother's great-grandfather had three wives, my father's great-grandfather had four. My family tree is like a diagram of the heart: all lines come from one organ.

—*Natasha Ahanin*

Family vacation. Some vacation sitting in the backseat of a 'seventy-two Ford Country Squire station wagon, with a flatulent sheepdog and my brother chanting, "I know you are, but what am I?" I know if you don't leave me alone you're going to be bludgeoned to death in your sleeping bag. Which, by the way, is flammable.

—*Joel Warshaw*

I told my mother-in-law that my house was her house, and she said, "Get the hell off my property."

— *Joan Rivers*

Older Jewish relatives can get away with murder. If they forget the name of something, they can make up a word that sounds like Yiddish. "Darling, pass me the . . . *huucch*. No, that's the *smeklinbach*."

— *Billy Crystal*

After watching the Kevorkian trial I asked my father, "Do you think family should have the right to withdraw life support on a loved one?" He said, "It depends on which kid."

— *Hugh Fink*

Fashion

I base my fashion taste on what doesn't itch.

— *Gilda Radner*

The suit is the universal business outfit for men. I don't know why it projects this image of power. "We'd better do what this guy says, his pants match his jacket!"

— *Jerry Seinfeld*

If high heels were so wonderful, men would be wearing them.

—*Sue Grafton*

Put heterosexual men in charge of fashion. Ladies, you'll never need to read *Vogue* magazine again. Here's the only outfit you'll need: miniskirt, high heels, bare midriff. Evening wear? Fishnet stockings and French-cut panties. Trust me, darlings, you'll be fabulous.

—*Dennis Miller*

There are weird rules for girls, we get all the uncomfortable crap. We get all the S and M clothes, like the high heels that make us easier to hunt.

—*Sue Murphy*

Fat

Americans are too damn fat. At one time I weighed 360 pounds, because I'm a practical guy. When you can buy two Big Macs for two bucks, it becomes cost efficient to be a fat bastard.

—*Jim Wyatt*

You thin people invite us over and say, "Come on in, sit on this concrete sofa. Or try our new steel-reinforced chair." I always head straight for the wicker.

—*Louie Anderson*

You know you're fat when you can pinch an inch on your forehead.

—*John Mendoza*

The National Association for Fat Acceptance had a conference in Boston. They said they wanted to be recognized for who they are, and be accepted by everyone, but they draw the line at singing "We Are the World."

—*Bill Maher*

Father

I bought my father an answering machine. He still hasn't figured out how to leave an outgoing message. You call my father's house . . . *ring, ring, ring, click*, "Goddamn it, Mary, how in the hell do you use this stupid piece of shit? Come over here and look and see if you can help me with the . . . *beep*!"

—*Rosie O'Donnell*

Last year my father adopted one of those Save the Children, and now he compares me to his adopted child. "Why can't you be like your sister Kee Kee? Kee Kee dug an irrigation ditch for a whole village. What the hell are you doing with your life?"

—*Corey Kahane*

My father carries around the picture of the kid who came with his wallet.

—*Rodney Dangerfield*

My dad is one of those Mr. Fix-it guys. Eight o'clock Sunday morning he'd be locked down in the basement with the power tools. *Mmmroaroor, roaroor.* "Dad, what are you doing down there?" "Making breakfast." My sister got married, we had to lead him into the church with a broken toaster.

—*Mike Rowe*

My dad went back to college and we're all so proud of him. Except when he comes home from a keg party and pees out the window.

—*Brian Kiley*

Dad was a kidder. Whenever I misbehaved, he'd bury me in the backyard. Only up to my waist, but you get dizzy with all the blood rushing to your head.

—*Emo Philips*

I want a guy just like my dad, who orders dentures through the mail, and takes great pride in the fact that his eyebrows meet.

—*Judy Tenuta*

My father is like me, he needs glasses to see, but he never wears them. He said, "Son, I'm watching the Miss America Pageant, they have eight-hundred numbers just in case you want to ask one of those fine girls on a date." I said, "Dad, you're watching *America's Most Wanted.*"

—*Robert Murray*

You know that saying, "Give a man a fish and he will eat for a day. Teach him how to fish and he will eat for life"? Here's what my mother used to say about my father, "Give that man ten dollars and he will drink for a day. Give that man a job, and he will hate you for life."

—*Jim Rez*

All fathers are intimidating, because they're fathers. Once a man has children, his attitude is, "To hell with the world, I can make my own people. I'll eat whenever I want, I'll wear whatever I want, and I'll create whoever I want."

—*Jerry Seinfeld*

My father's mind is going. He called me and said, "When I get up to go to the bathroom in the middle of the night, I don't have to turn on the light. It goes on automatically when I start, and goes off when I stop." I said, "Dad, you're peeing in the fridge."

—*Jonathan Katz*

I love my dad because even though he has Alzheimer's, he still remembers the important things. He can't remember my name, but last week he told me exactly how much money I owe him.

—*Thyra Lees-Smith*

Now that I'm a dad, I'm sure my father is laughing in his grave. I used to ask my father, "Dad, where did all those wrinkles come from on your face?" "From you, your little brother, and your goddamn sister."

—*Jack Coen*

My dad died in 1990 and I've had the same dream every night since. I die and go down a tunnel of light, to a room filled with light. My dad walks in and says, "Joe! Did you leave all these lights on?"

—*Joe Ditzel*

Feet

I bought Odor-Eaters. They ate for half an hour, and then threw up.

—*Howie Mandel*

Fight

I got into a fight one time with a really big guy, and he said, "I'm going to mop the floor with your face." I said, "You'll be sorry." He said, "Oh yeah? Why?" I said, "Well, you won't be able to get into the corners very well."

—*Emo Philips*

Fire

We had fire drills in my house, so that in case of a fire we each had a special duty. My father had to get the pets, my mother grabbed the jewelry, my brother ran out to get help. They told me to save the washer and dryer.

—*Ellen DeGeneres*

Fired

I've been fired a few times in my life. And that's fine. In a lot of cases, it's only a little worse than getting hired.

—*Laura Kightlinger*

I was actually fired as a Denny's dishwasher. They didn't even know how to fire me, they had never done it in the history of Denny's. They just sent me out to take out the garbage, and locked the door behind me. I'm like, "Let me in." And they're like, "Go to Wendy's!"

—*Mitch Fatel*

I used to work at the unemployment office. I hated that job because when they fired me, I still had to show up at work the next day.

—*Wally Wang*

Fishing

I used to go fishing until one day it struck me: you can buy fish. What the hell am I doing in a boat at 4:30 in the morning? If I want a hamburger, I don't track cattle down.

—*Kenny Rogerson*

There's a fine line between fishing and standing on the shore looking like an idiot.

—*Steven Wright*

Flirting

I finally figured out this flirting thing. My best friend is legally blind. She walks into a room and looks around trying to focus. Looks away, for some recognizable reference point. Looks back, squints, you know, that sexy look guys love? Then flutters her eyelashes in frustration, and guys drop to the floor in worship. Thing is, she doesn't know it, can't see. She leaves. Guys think she's stuck up, and there I am. It's good to befriend the handicapped.

—*Johnnye Jones Gibson*

Flying

The major airlines have unveiled long-promised plans to improve customer satisfaction. United plans to purchase more luggage scanners, Delta plans to install a toll-free number for complaints, and USAir says they're going to try extra hard not to crash so much.

—*Craig Kilborn*

When you're taking a flight, if you miss it, that's it. No airline goes, "Missed the flight? We have a cannon leaving in about ten minutes. So all right, let's aim it . . . where are you going? Now, make sure you get out of the net immediately, because we shoot the luggage in right after you."

—*Jerry Seinfeld*

The stewardess comes running out of the cockpit, and says, "The pilot just passed out! Can somebody fly the plane?" Nobody else raised their hand, so I figured I'd take a shot at it. It took me almost four hours just to get it off the runway.

—*James Leemer*

My wife began to breast-feed our baby to relieve his ear pressure during takeoff. Which, I understand, hands down beats the hell out of chewing gum.

—*Paul Reiser*

I sit in the cheap seats, and the flight attendant goes, "Would you like to read a *Wall Street Journal*?" If I could read the *Wall Street Journal*, I wouldn't be sitting in coach. We would like the *Enquirer* back here, we're the morons on this flight. Smart people up front, dumb people in the back. They have computers, we have Nintendo. They're closing business deals, we're opening beers.

—*Kathleen Madigan*

I don't like to fly, so I took a bus from London to Boston. Do you know how much that costs? I never had so much change in my hands.

—*Steven Wright*

I'd like to ask all the airlines just to do one thing. Keep the planes intact in the air. I don't mind economy class, it's patio seating I have a problem with. Get all the people who make the sandwiches, and have them inspect the rivets. We will pack a lunch.

—*Rick Ducommun*

I'm terrified of dying in a plane crash. I hate the thought that peanuts would be my last meal.

—*Tanya Luckerath*

Hey, I don't get respect from anyone. American Airlines, they thanked me for flying United.

—*Rodney Dangerfield*

Food

You ever wonder if illiterate people get the full effect of alphabet soup?

—*John Mendoza*

Two new medical studies report that beer can stop ulcers, and pizza can actually stop prostate problems. Beer and pizza are healthy for you. You know what that means, parents? Now you can write off your kid's college as a medical expense.

—*Jay Leno*

British scientists have found a substance that dulls the appetite. It's called British food.

—*Johnny Robish*

I love greasy food. A chili dog with cheese and bacon. That's a power meal, marches right down your throat, "Follow me boys, we're going to the heart! You, chili come with me, we're going to the colon. Quick, before he gets home!"

—*Drew Carey*

In a move to shake up sales, Campbell's soups is redesigning its label after 102 years. The new label features a photo of soup in a bowl, which will come as a revelation to the millions of consumers who ate their soup out of a hat. Not changing is the Quick Recipe on the back. For those times when you have to cook, but hate the person you're cooking for.

—*Jon Stewart*

Starbucks announced that they're raising the price of their coffee by ten cents a cup. That's right. Starbucks said they had to raise prices, 'cause they don't have all of our money yet.

—*Conan O'Brien*

I bought a box of animal crackers, and it said on it, "Do not eat if seal is broken." So I opened up the box, and sure enough . . .

—*Brian Kiley*

I hate how my grocery store is always rearranging things. Product placement is what they call it. The other day I had just enough time to run in for a jar of spaghetti sauce and couldn't find it. But I learned something, my kids will eat peanut butter on anything. That night, we had Skippy fettucine.

—*Eileen Courtney*

I just love Chinese food. It's immediate gratification. You call, give them the order, you hang up, and *bing bong,* the doorbell rings. It's like they have a helicopter and a wok, and they just lower it to you.

—*Lew Schneider*

Scientists say that chocolate affects your brain the same way sex does. Which means that after they eat a Snickers, guys roll over and go to sleep. And women ask the wrapper, "What are you thinking?"

—*Jim Wyatt*

Cured ham? No thanks, pal. Cured of what? What if it has a relapse on my plate?

—*Tommy Sledge*

I've spent a lifetime becoming a fast-food connoisseur. The other day I was in a fast-food joint and someone ordered a fish sandwich and a strawberry shake. I just looked over and said, "Hmmmph . . . a red shake? With seafood?"

—*Vince Maranto*

I come from a family where gravy is considered a beverage.

—*Erma Bombeck*

I used to love fast food, but that stuff will kill you. Why do you think that fast-food joints and emergency rooms are both open twenty-four hours a day? And they both have drive-throughs.

—*Joel Warshaw*

Have you ever seen these places that feature fish sandwiches? I always think, "Well, that's kind of general." I wouldn't order something called a meat sandwich. At least not without a couple of follow-up questions: "Does anyone know where this meat came from? Are any of the waitresses missing?"

—*George Carlin*

When I was a kid my mother would make chopped liver for company, and I thought, "Who wants to eat liver?" That's the organ that filters out all the crap you eat. I'd look at the liver on my plate and worry, "That could have been an alcoholic cow."

—*Joel Warshaw*

At my lemonade stand I used to give the first glass away free and charge five dollars for the second glass. The refill contained the antidote.

—*Emo Philips*

Matzo is a Hebrew word meaning "flour baked with Elmer's glue."

—*Norman K.*

Why is McDonald's still counting? What is their ultimate goal? To have cows surrendering voluntarily? "We see the sign, we realize we have very little chance out there. We'd like to be a Happy Meal, if at all possible."

—*Jerry Seinfeld*

I'm eating microwave dinners like crazy. How much salt is in them? My blood pressure is one thousand over ninety. I've got deer following me around.

—*Evan Davis*

I will not eat oysters. I want my food dead. Not sick, not wounded, dead.

—*Woody Allen*

If I dine out I want outrageously obscene amounts of food, and upscale restaurants rarely provide this. The quantities I'm referring to are best found on a supermarket shelf, taken home, and ingested quickly and shamefully, like the good Lord and the media intended.

—*Janeane Garofalo*

I got food poisoning today. I don't know when I'll use it.

—*Steven Wright*

I can't believe how many different kinds of soda there are now. I ordered one caffeine free, low sodium, no artificial flavor, and got a glass of water.

—*Robert Murray*

Most turkeys taste better the day after. My mother's tasted better the day before.

—*Rita Rudner*

Friend

When I was a girl I only had two friends, and they were imaginary. And they would only play with each other.

—*Rita Rudner*

He's the kind of friend who will always be there when he needs you.

—*Adam Christing*

My best friend ran away with my wife. And let me tell you, I really miss him.

—*Henny Youngman*

Some people think my friend George is weird, because he has sideburns behind his ears. I think George is weird because he has false teeth, with braces on them.

—*Steven Wright*

She's my best friend. She thinks I'm too thin, and I think she's a natural blond.

—*Carrie Snow*

You got friends, then you've got your best friend. Big difference. To me, a friend's a guy who will help you move. A best friend's a guy who will help you move—a body. That's how I look at it.

—*Dave Attell*

Funeral

I had a friend who was a clown. When he died, all his friends went to the funeral in one car.

—*Steven Wright*

The purpose of a funeral service is to comfort the living. It is important at a funeral to display excessive grief. This will show others how kindhearted and loving you are, and their improved opinion of you will be very comforting.

—*P. J. O'Rourke*

The guy who invented the hokey-pokey just died. It was a weird funeral. First, they put his left leg in . . .

—*Irv Gilman*

With my wife I don't get no respect at all. I told her when I die, I want to be cremated. She's planning a barbecue.

—*Rodney Dangerfield*

Fur

They're obsessed with fur in San Francisco—"I'm going to step over this disgusting homeless person, to pet this cute little kitty."

—*Greg Proops*

For our anniversary, I got my wife one of those fur coat kits. A Velcro coat with a hundred gerbils.

—*Tom Arnold*

We hate the idea of killing baby seals and foxes and minks, but there'd be no problem if someone showed up in a nice full-length rat coat. Or a double-breasted weasel jacket. It's the same way we treat each other. Penalize the unattractive, idolize the cute.

—*Paul Reiser*

Furniture

I don't have any furniture in my apartment yet, but my grandmother said she'll give me some of hers. So now my apartment is going to look like the set of *Pirates of Penzance*.

—*Brock Cohen*

My grandfather had a special rocking chair built that would lean forward rather than backward, so that he could fake interest in any conversation.

—*Steven Wright*

I just bought a leather couch. They should tell you that when it's warm and you sit on a leather couch in your underwear, when you stand up the whole couch comes with you.

—*Rondell Sheridan*

My mother had plastic slipcovers on the couch. When I was six years old, I put a ham sandwich in it. When I found it last week, it was still fresh.

—*Danny McWilliams*

Gambling

I'll tell you how to beat the gambling in Las Vegas. When you get off the airplane, walk right into the propeller.

—*Henny Youngman*

In Vegas, I got into a long argument with the man at the roulette wheel over what I considered to be an odd number.

—*Steven Wright*

I don't get no respect. I joined Gamblers Anonymous. They gave me two to one I don't make it.

—*Rodney Dangerfield*

Gas Station

In Beverly Hills now, when you pull into the gas station there are two guys in the booth. The attendant, and the loan officer.

—*Jay Leno*

My gas station had a sign that read, "Please pay with your smallest bill." So I gave them the white dollar bill from my Monopoly set. The cops caught up with me a couple blocks later, but I was in luck. I also had the "Get out of Jail Free" card.

—*Kate Zannoni*

I saw a sign at a gas station. It said, "Help Wanted." There was another sign below it that said, "Self Service." So I hired myself, then I made myself the boss. I gave myself a raise. I paid myself. Then I quit.

—*Steven Wright*

Gay

I was definitely a gay kid. My tree house had a breakfast nook.

—*Bob Smith*

As women, as lesbians and gay men, we are denied certain very basic human rights. The last time most people in this society cared about my rights, I was a fetus. And the next time they'll care about my rights, is when I die and come back as a whale.

—*Sarah Citron*

Here is a little tip for all of you. Don't come out to your father in a moving vehicle.

—*Kate Clinton*

I thank God for creating gay men. Because if it wasn't for them, us fat women would have no one to dance with.

—*Roseanne*

If homosexuality is a disease, let's all call in queer to work. "Hello, can't work today. Still queer."

—*Robin Tyler*

Jerry Falwell thinks that homosexuals are out to recruit guys, to lead them into dangerous and life-threatening situations. That's the army, Jerry! Homosexuality, you gotta audition. And it's grueling! All those lines from old movies, the antiques, the fabrics. And, of course, you've gotta do the whole thing while dancing. Then there's the physical.

—*Atom*

In college I experimented with heterosexuality: I slept with a straight guy. I was really drunk.

—*Bob Smith*

I'm a big queen when I'm flying, I'm always nervous on planes. Not of crashing, but of my skin drying out.

—*Frank Maya*

I read in the newspaper that a big earthen dyke crumbled in Utah. Don't laugh, I knew her.

—*Karen Ripley*

Gays are not allowed to march in the St. Patrick's Day parade, but someone from the Irish Republican Army did. Now I ask you, who is more dangerous? A group who has been known to blow up buses, or people who know all the lyrics to Stephen Sondheim musicals?

—*Joy Behar*

Geography

I was in Alaska. I was there for two days and six nights. It was so cold, I saw a dog wearing a cat.

—*Wendy Liebman*

I grew up in Tucson, Arizona, where it's 120 degrees in the summer. One day our dog burst into flames. We thought we were going have to start a backfire on the cat.

—*Garry Shandling*

Australia is like Arkansas, with a beach.

—*Greg Proops*

I went to Australia, and those aborigines are so backward, they don't even have casinos. What kind of native people don't have casinos? That's what life was like before the white man: hunting, gathering, and gambling.

—*Norman K.*

I like California pretty much. I especially like California when it's not moving. The idea of the ground opening up and sucking me in is not my idea of a good time. I already dated someone like that.

—*Matina Bevis*

When I was crossing the border into Canada, they asked if I had any firearms with me. I said, "What do you need?"

—*Steven Wright*

I used to live in Edmonton, Canada. There was a big sign downtown that said, "Jesus Saves!" And somebody spray-painted underneath, "and Gretzky scores on the rebound."

—*Joe Ditzel*

Fast food is everywhere. I was in China, and the biggest restaurant chain was Kentucky Fried Chicken. I think they still used the same eleven herbs and spices, but that was the first time I was ever asked if I wanted my order declawed.

—*Jim Wyatt*

It's a good thing I didn't grow up in Germany. There a D cup is like a trainer bra.

—*Tanya Luckerath*

I spend a lot of time in England because I like a country where I'm considered the best-looking person. In England, God bless that dinky island, it's, "Look at him! He has all his teeth, and his ears are in proportion to his head!"

—*Greg Proops*

I just got back from visiting my father in Iran. It's difficult there for a woman. I had to cover my body and my hair, and I had to do so on the plane before we landed. The stewardesses were really nice, "Peanuts, ginger ale . . . black cloak?" They have prostitutes in Iran, but it's a little different. "Oooh, you're so hot. Would you like to see my . . . ear?"

—*Natasha Ahanin*

I went to Israel and I tell you, boy, they're cocky. God was born there, so there's no talking to those people. I'm from Jersey and we've got Springsteen, but that's different. You get off the plane, and it's, "Welcome to Israel, the Holy Land." Oh, great, I'm from America, Home of the Whopper.

—*Jon Stewart*

You can't smoke in a restaurant in Los Angeles. Which is mildly ironic, considering that you can't breathe the air outside a restaurant in Los Angeles.

—*Greg Proops*

In Israel it's traditional to throw water as your guests exit, for good luck. So my mother-in-law always throws a cup of water at me and my fiancé when we leave her house. Last night she turned the hose on us. Next week I'm bringing a squirt gun and telling her, "This is an American tradition, Mom."

—*Stephanie Schiern*

Being from Kentucky, I'm not impressed by the Star Wars plot twists. Darth Vader is Luke's father, big deal. In a small town, everyone knows who your father is, and where he ran off to. "Son of a gun took up with some no-count, floozy evil empire. Force, my ass. He was always a bad apple." The real surprise would be if Darth Vader turned out to be Luke's father, *and* his cousin.

—*Lesley Wake*

Los Angeles is a city that makes you feel like shit about yourself twenty-four hours a day, so I've been thinking about getting breast implants. Not because I need them, but because I live in L.A. But if I get implants, I want people to know I spent the money, so I'm thinking of getting four. Two up, two down. Now that's fancy.

—*Cathryn Michon*

I was pulled over in Massachusetts for reckless driving. The judge asked me, "Do you know what the punishment for drunk driving in this state is?" I said, "I don't know. Reelection to the Senate?"

—*Emo Philips*

I'm from Milwaukee, home of beer, Harley-Davidson motorcycles, and per capita the most overweight people on the face of the earth. UFOs won't land there because they can't get anyone in the spaceship and still have power to take off.

—*Dobie Maxwell*

I'm from Minnesota, such an embarrassing place. Jesse Ventura is governor, that's really all you need to know. When I was a kid I used to fantasize that I was from somewhere really glamorous and exciting, like South Dakota.

—*Cathryn Michon*

In New York my apartment had every kind of insect, every bug imaginable. I had serious rodents. Mice in tap shoes. Rats in pimp outfits, "Gimme some cheese, bitch."

—*Billy Crystal*

There was an item in the paper today. A lion got loose in the Central Park Zoo. And was severely mauled.

—*Bob Newhart*

A man died on the New York subway and his body rode around for five hours before anybody noticed. Everything is fine now, the proper officials were notified, and they were able to put the body in the East River where it belongs.

—*Conan O'Brien*

New York is an exciting town where something is happening all the time, most of it unsolved.

—*Johnny Carson*

New York City is expecting twenty thousand potholes from this winter's blizzard. City officials are concerned that there may not be enough streets to accommodate them.

—*Johnny Robish*

New York now leads the world's great cities in the number of people around whom you shouldn't make a move.

—*David Letterman*

I'm a New Yorker who moved to California, and now I live in Ohio. Each place has a different outlook on life. To New Yorkers life is a war, in California life is a beach. In the Midwest life is a brewski.

—*Karen Williams*

Ohio is an old Indian word. It means, "I'm so bored my head hurts."

—*Joe Ditzel*

When I first moved to San Francisco it was foggy, rainy, and cold. At first I thought it's sort of romantic, I'll break up an old chair for kindling, buy a bottle of wine, and sit in front of the fire for the day. Two months later . . . a hopeless alcoholic, with no furniture.

—*Paula Poundstone*

I was raised in Utah, and Salt Lake is very . . . Caucasian. I was at this restaurant one time, and the hostess called for the White party. Everybody stood up.

—*Natasha Ahanin*

I'm going to write a book about the South. I'm going to call it *When Beautiful Places Happen to Bad People*.

—*Brett Butler*

I tellin' ya, I get no respect. When I was in Switzerland, I got an obscene yodel.

—*Rodney Dangerfield*

Firefighters descended on the Blue Ridge Mountains in Tennessee when smoke could be seen from over thirty miles away. They were relieved to find that the source of the smoke was just another Willie Nelson camping trip.

—*Craig Kilborn*

In Tulsa, restaurants have signs that say, "Sorry, we're open."

—*Roseanne*

Washington, D.C., is no longer an honored and revered institution commanding the respect of its republic, but a soap opera circus, a tabloid dartboard, a Hollywood with better acting, and a bemusement park where the rides are four years long, and the popcorn is a billion dollars a bucket.

—*Dennis Miller*

A hurricane, the worst in decades, also hit up north. Even in Washington, D.C., residents had to seek out fixed, immovable structures like basements and Elizabeth Dole's hair.

—*Bill Maher*

I like the West. That's where men are men and women are women, and it's hard to beat a combination like that.

—*Milton Berle*

Girlfriend

Last week I saw what was left of my ex-girlfriend at the grocery store. She'd pierced her nose, bleached her hair, and had lip, cheek, and breast implants. She was so artificial, I could barely recognize her from two feet away. It made me wonder, "Why couldn't she have looked like that when *we* were going out?"

—*Brock Cohen*

You can't please everybody. Like, I have a girlfriend. My girlfriend to me is the most wonderful, most remarkable person in the world. That's to me. But to my wife . . .

—*Jackie Mason*

I don't have a girlfriend. But I do know a woman who'd be mad at me for saying that.

—*Mitch Hedberg*

Glasses

People always want to try on my glasses. That's rude. I don't go to people with hairpieces, "Hey, let me try on your wig. Let me sit in your wheelchair. Oh my God, you are *so* crippled."

—*Jim Gaffigan*

The first time I went outside with my new trifocals, I took a three-mile walk through the lobby of my ophthalmologist's building, climbed a five-foot curb, and then met an autograph seeker who happened to be a giant eyeball. "Mr. Cosby, could I have your autograph?" "Yes, yes! Just don't eat me!"

—*Bill Cosby*

God

I think a lot of people believe in God, just in case. You don't want to be in heaven going, "Isn't there some kind of community service I could do?"

—*Mark Maron*

I'm Jewish, but I was raised superstitious. I don't actually believe in God. I do believe, though, that you shouldn't step on the cracks in the sidewalk.

—*Jonathan Katz*

God has got some hard rules. "Turn the other cheek." You might slap me, I might turn the other cheek. But when I come back around, your ass better not be there.

—*Steve Harvey*

In the beginning there was nothing. God said, "Let there be light!" And there was light. There was still nothing, but you could see it a whole lot better.

—*Ellen DeGeneres*

God is love, but get it in writing.

—*Gypsy Rose Lee*

If a kid asks where rain comes from, I think a cute thing to tell him is God is crying. And if he asks why God is crying, another cute thing to tell him is, "Probably because of something you did."

—*Emo Philips*

A lawsuit was dismissed against God. Somebody in Syracuse sued God for not giving him guitar-playing skills, and not bringing back his pigeon from the dead. But the judge said you can't sue God. Because if you do, the next thing they'll start to challenge Microsoft.

—*Bill Maher*

I fear that one day I'll meet God, he'll sneeze, and I won't know what to say.

—*Ronnie Shakes*

Golf

My dad's a golfer. Well, not really, he watches it on TV. But it takes the same amount of energy to get a sweat going on that vinyl seat after nine hours.

—*Mike Rowe*

I don't rent a golf cart. I don't need one. Where I hit the ball, I can use public transportation.

—*Gene Perret*

Grandchildren

I'm not even married yet and my future in-laws are already pressuring me to produce grandsons. Their motto is, "We're not losing a son, we're gaining a uterus."

—*Stephanie Schiern*

Grandfather

I only have one grandpa. We call him Grandpa Alive. He still beats me at checkers, but I kick his ass at full-contact karate.

—*Dave Attell*

My grandfather is hard of hearing, he needs to read lips. I don't mind him reading lips, but he uses those yellow highlighters.

—*Brian Kiley*

My grandfather, and the talks. The We Didn't Have Anything in the Old Days talk. "What happiness? We didn't have happiness in the old days. We were miserable, and we liked it."

—*Billy Crystal*

When I was little, my grandfather used to make me stand in a closet for five minutes without moving. He said it was elevator practice.

—*Steven Wright*

I'll always remember the last words of my grandfather, who said, "A truck!"

—*Emo Philips*

Grandmother

Call waiting. My grandmother says, "I've got call waiting. You call and the line is busy, you wait till I get through."

—*Sinbad*

My grandmother is eighty-five years old and she's starting to lose her memory. Everybody's upset about it except me, because I got eight checks for my birthday from her. Hey, that's forty bucks.

—*Tom Arnold*

My grandmother was a very tough woman. She buried three husbands. Two of them were just napping.

—*Rita Rudner*

My nana, ninety years old and still driving. Not with me, that would be stupid.

—*Tim Allen*

My grandmother's brain was dead, but her heart was still beating. It was the first time we ever had a Democrat in the family.

—*Emo Philips*

Greeting Card

The clearest indication of the complexity of modern relationships is the greeting cards that are blank on the inside. It's like the card companies say, "We give up, you think of something. For seventy-five cents, it's not worth us getting involved."

—*Jerry Seinfeld*

Gun Control

Last year in this country there were more people killed as a result of firearms than as a result of automobile accidents. A trend that will continue until we can develop a more accurate automobile.

—*Jonathan Katz*

The Centers for Disease Control report that guns are now the second leading cause of premature death in America, just behind AIDS. So, if you must have unprotected sex, don't use a gun.

—*Johnny Robish*

Guns don't kill people. It's those bullets ripping through the body.

—*Eddie Izzard*

We don't need no gun control, we need bullet control. Bullets should cost five thousand dollars, then people would think before they killed somebody. "Man, I would blow your head off, if I could afford it. I'm going to get me another job, save my money. You better hope I can't get no bullets on layaway."

—*Chris Rock*

You want gun control? Get rid of metal detectors around the Capitol building. Take away Secret Service protection for politicians. By next week the worst thing you'll have to worry about is drive-by shoutings. Which, I might add, are protected by the First Amendment.

—*Dennis Miller*

Why does man kill? He kills for food. And not only food, frequently there must be a beverage.

—*Woody Allen*

The NRA says that every man and woman has the right to bear arms. But the Constitution was written when your nearest neighbor was two hundred miles away, and it took you thirty minutes to load. If the founding fathers knew you could get AK-47s, they might have phrased it a little differently: "A man has the right to bear a musket . . ."

—*Sinbad*

Some nut in Texas went into a church and shot people. But Charlton Heston pointed out that this never would have happened if the minister had been armed. And, never missing a beat, Congress insisted that churches begin posting the Ten Commandments.

—*Bill Maher*

I saw Charlton Heston on TV defending his right to remain violent. But I found myself yelling, "Hey, Charlie! Who shot your toupee?" He's the head of the NRA, you'd assume he'd be a great shot. So how come his toupee looks like roadkill?

—*Atom*

I'm all for hunters having guns. Or anything else that increases the odds of two rednecks blowing each other's heads off.

—*Bobcat Goldthwait*

Gym

My favorite machine at the gym is the vending machine.

—*Caroline Rhea*

Have you been to the gym lately? Boy, some of those guys overdevelop. If your neck is as wide as your head, take a day off.

—*Margaret Smith*

The StairMaster at my gym is scary, it tells you how many floors you've climbed. The guy next to me must have been depressed because he climbed fifty-two floors, walked to the edge, and jumped to his death.

—*Joe Ditzel*

Why would anyone want to go to a place called a family fitness center? Why should your family burn off their pent-up energies at a gym, when you can all accomplish the same thing for free at home with a series of ugly, confrontational shouting matches?

—*Dennis Miller*

I worked out at this really fancy health club. They had a spiral StairMaster.

—*Wendy Liebman*

My gym has two-pound weights. If you're using two-pound weights, how did you even open the door to the gym? What's your dream? To pump up and open your mail?

—*Dave Attell*

I had to cancel my gym membership, because they won't let me smoke at the juice bar. Hey, I bench-pressed an anorexic from step class, I deserve that coffin nail.

—*Cindee Weiss*

I never work out. I only go to the gym once a year—to renew. When I get the urge to exercise, I just lie down till it passes.

—*Le Maire*

Why are we so careful about locking up our dirty towels and smelly jockstraps? What exactly is the black market for these disgusting gym clothes? I'll give my car to any guy in a short red jacket in front of a restaurant, but for my stinking, putrefied workout clothes I've got one of these locks you could put a bullet through.

—*Jerry Seinfeld*

Hair

I got a bad haircut recently. It was a haircut that actually redefined head trauma.

—*Cindee Weiss*

Why did Mom insist on cutting my hair herself until I was fourteen? She had a home haircut kit that looked like Mengele's briefcase, and the barber skills of Dr. Leatherface brandishing a flowbee. Looks good, Mom. If my school ever does a stage production of *Sling Blade,* this haircut makes me look like Karl's stupider friend, who couldn't get laid with Brad Pitt's dick.

—*Dennis Miller*

When I was in college I shaved my head, mostly to spite my mother. And I really went all out: I did it in her bathroom, used her razor—practiced on her cat. And it was the holidays in my little Ohio town, so I was sporting all my mother's Christmas presents. So picture this: shaved head, teddy bear turtleneck, Christmas tree sweater. I looked like Telly Savalas went to Sears.

—*Ann Oelschlager*

I used to go to old-fashioned barbershops, because they were cheap. They have pictures on the wall of all these different hairstyles. But no matter which you pick, everyone comes out with the same damn cut, looking like Pugsley from the Addams Family.

—*Joey Gallinal*

I hate the fact that I'm losing my hair, but it's genetic. I've figured a way around this family curse; I'm adopting. I wouldn't care if my child were the illegitimate bastard of Charles Manson. Because you've got to admit, before he carved that swastika into his forehead, Charlie had a great head of hair.

—*Joel Warshaw*

You never see anyone anymore with the little Hitler mustache. He ruined that look forever, it's good he chose such a lame one. Imagine if Hitler had gone with the big Elvis sideburns? The tragedy would be that Elvis couldn't have had them, and he might have gone with the little mustache.

—*Al Lubel*

Handicapped

Whenever I see a handicapped parking sticker, I get the hell out of there. If they're handicapped, why are they driving? Apparently the geniuses at the DMV can overrule a doctor. But when they give out mental handicapped stickers, you'll really see me move. A schizophrenic hits my car, I'm gonna be pissed, no matter which of his personalities did it.

—*Joel Warshaw*

Hanging Out

Hanging out with your friends late, that's when it all happens. Go home a little early, big mistake. You get that call the next day, "Ten minutes after you left, the Spice Girls broke in and had sex with everyone. Even the fat kid wearing the Babylon Five T-shirt got a little."

—*Dave Attell*

I don't go out with my single friends anymore, because I never have any fun. Go to a club, a guy comes over, says, "Can I buy you a drink?" "No, oh no, she's *married*." Yeah, I'm married, but I'm thirsty. Why don't you shut the hell up, and let me have a free drink?

—*Wanda Sykes-Hall*

Health

I'm into health. Just let me give you a quick hint. Stay away from any substance that's white. Sugar, flour, milk, salt, heroin, cocaine. And of course, the most dangerous thing of all: white people.

—*Richard Belzer*

I know I need some kind of athletic activity in my life, so I subscribed to a couple of health magazines. There's nothing better than kicking back with a cigarette, a Budweiser, and *Prevention* magazine . . . and reading about what nicotine, alcohol, and sloth will do to me. The anxiety alone raises my heart rate.

—*Cindee Weiss*

Any kind of physical test I want to do well. Remember those hearing tests in school? I was trying to hear so hard, I wanted them to say to me afterwards, "We think you have something close to super-hearing. You heard a cotton ball touching a piece of felt. We're sending the results to Washington. We'd like you to meet the president."

—*Jerry Seinfeld*

According to a brand-new study, kissing may boost the immune system and help you live longer. That's why every time I go to the doctor, I ask him to slip me the tongue.

—*Conan O'Brien*

Women are more realistic when it comes to health. You ever notice that when men get sick, they blame it on the last thing they ate? A couple piña coladas, a plate of cheese fries, a steak, fried chicken, big wedge of chocolate cake, and he finishes with one of those dinner mints. Gets in the car and goes, "Ohhh, I shouldn't have eaten that mint! *What was in that mint?*"

—*Jay Leno*

Hell

How bad do you have to be before they take you to hell? Maybe there's a bargaining period. I could promise to do volunteer work. There must be subchambers in hell, different levels. Rooms at street level, rooms with air conditioners. Rooms with a view of the inferno. Rooms where they automatically bring ketchup when you order fries.

—*Louie Anderson*

I love Christians who tell me something sweet and Christian, like "You're going to hell!" It's not hard for me to picture gay hell. "The scorching wind from the fiery pit messed up my hair, there's no mousse? No blow-dryer? This is hell! There's nothing on TV but *Hee Haw*. My furniture is from Levitz! I'm living in a trailer park! Aaaah!"

—*Danny McWilliams*

I grew up in a non-Jewish community where a lot of people would tell me I was going to hell because I'm Jewish. So I wondered, what would hell be like? All the assholes will be there. It'll be really hot. And if the Jews are there, you'll have the entertainment industry. It'll be a lot like living in Los Angeles.

— *Stephanie Schiern*

Highway

My house is on the median strip of a highway. You don't really notice, except I have to leave the driveway doing sixty miles per hour.

—*Steven Wright*

History

Like Joan of Arc, my life ended at nineteen. In my case, I married.

—*Shannon Ireland*

Gays started the Renaissance. It was probably two gay guys at a party saying, "Wouldn't it be fun to make religious paintings of hot naked guys, and sell them to churches? Oh, that would be a hoot!"

—*Bob Smith*

The lie is that the Pilgrims were seeking religious freedom in the New World. The Pilgrims were asked to leave England because they got tired of those right-wing psycho-Christians bumming people out and wearing buckles on their heads. "Hey, why don't you freaky weirdos get into a rickety little boat, sail to a new world, and commit genocide on the indigenous people? Have a witch trial. We'll be over here enjoying the Renaissance."

—*Greg Proops*

Do you think when they asked George Washington for his ID, he just took out a quarter?

—*Steven Wright*

Based on what you know about him in history books, what do you think Abraham Lincoln would be doing if he were alive today? 1. Writing his memoirs of the Civil War. 2. Advising the president. 3. Desperately clawing at the inside of his coffin.

—*David Letterman*

People always ask me, "Where were you when Kennedy was shot?" Well, I don't have an alibi.

—*Emo Philips*

There's only one living member of the Warren Commission, and that's Gerald Ford. He's also the dumbest member of the Warren Commission. Coincidence?

—*Richard Belzer*

It's been twenty-five years since Nixon's resignation, and a lot has changed with the Republican Party since then. For example, today's family values. Republicans back then were still on their first wives.

—*Bill Maher*

During the mid-1980s dairy farmers decided there was too much cheap milk at the supermarket. So the government bought and slaughtered 1.6 million dairy cows. How come the government never does anything like this with lawyers?

—*P. J. O'Rourke*

Three teachers hiking in remote British Columbia stumbled upon the remains of an ancient man trapped in an ice floe. At first, experts weren't sure just how old the man was. But, fortunately, his well-preserved body was still wearing his Class of 4309 B.C. high school ring.

—*Craig Kilborn*

Holidays

My mom wanted to know why I never get home for the holidays. I said, "Because I can't get Delta to wait in the yard while I run in."

—*Margaret Smith*

I bought my brother some gift wrap for Christmas. I took it to the gift wrap department and told them to wrap it, but in a different print so he would know when to stop unwrapping.

—*Steven Wright*

My parents were cruel to me. I was about four years old when my dad asked me what I wanted for Christmas. I said, "I'd like a little dolly." Christmas Day he wheels in this tremendous metal thing. You ever try to dress one of those things?

—*Ellen DeGeneres*

When I was little my grandfather one Christmas gave me a box of broken glass. He gave my brother a box of Band-Aids, and said, "You two share."

—*Steven Wright*

My six-year-old nephew couldn't understand why I bought toys to give to a charity for poor kids. Couldn't those kids wait for Santa's free toys to come Christmas Day? I broke down and told him the truth, that Santa Claus is a Republican.

—*Brenda Pontiff*

Last Christmas I got no respect. In my stocking, I got an Odor-Eater.

—*Rodney Dangerfield*

The mayor of New York spent Christmas morning giving out free turkeys in Harlem. And then had the police tenderize the turkeys with their nightsticks.

—*Chris Rock*

I celebrated Thanksgiving in the traditional way. I invited everyone in my neighborhood to my house, we had an enormous feast. And then I killed them and took their land.

—*Jon Stewart*

I went to a Halloween party dressed as the Equator. People who walked toward me got warmer.

—*Steven Wright*

A guy comes down to Earth, takes your sins, dies, and comes back three days later. You believe in him, and go to heaven forever. How do you get from that to hide the eggs? Did Jesus have a problem with eggs? Did he go, "When I come back, if I see any eggs, the whole salvation thing is off"?

—*Jon Stewart*

I love Halloween, I never have any problem finding a car to borrow. I just dress up as a valet, and then stand in front of an expensive hotel, and say, "May I park your Porsche, sir?"

—*Robert Murray*

Last Thanksgiving I shot my own turkey. It was fun. That shotgun going, Blam! Blam! Everybody at the supermarket just staring. Why track them when I know where they are?

—*Kenny Rogerson*

We're having something a little different this year for Thanksgiving. Instead of a turkey, we're having a swan. You get more stuffing.

—*George Carlin*

Calista Flockhart, TV's Ally McBeal, celebrated Thanksgiving this year by eating half a crouton. And she washed it down by sucking on a Wet-Nap.

—*Chris Rock*

I'm from Canada, so Thanksgiving to me is just Thursday with more food. And I'm thankful for that.

—*Howie Mandel*

The mother of those sextuplets wanted to be home for Thanksgiving, and she got her wish. She said she wanted to be able to prepare the Thanksgiving feast herself, if she could find where she left that darn turkey baster.

—*Bill Maher*

On Presidents' Day you stay home and you don't do anything. Sounds like Vice Presidents' Day.

—*Jay Leno*

I wanted to make it really special on Valentine's Day, so I tied my boyfriend up. And for three solid hours I watched whatever I wanted to on TV.

—*Tracy Smith*

You know, Jews have great holidays. Like Yom Kippur, Jewish Day of Atonement. You don't eat for one day, all your sins are wiped clean for the whole year. Beat that with your Lent. Even in sin you're paying retail.

—*Jon Stewart*

My family is Jewish, so on holidays we eat these big, heavy, starchy meals. In honor of Jewish cooking, our next holiday will be called the Festival of Tums.

—*Fran Chernowsky*

Hollywood

I think I finally understand the Oscars. It's a chance for the movie industry to show people how boring television is.

—*Bill Maher*

I was watching the Academy Awards and noticed that when the camera panned the audience you could plainly see that the plastic surgeon's scalpel must have been working overtime. Maybe we should just call it the Night of a Hundred Scars.

—*Joy Behar*

They're going too far with the way they advertise movies. They figure we believe as long as someone involved with one hit movie contributes to a new one, that it will be worth seeing. It's like, "From the parking lot attendant who brought you *Independence Day,* and the janitor who worked on *Titanic,* comes *Star Trek Eighteen: The Brady Bunch Conquers Outer Space.*"

—*Robert Murray*

Homeless

My family was homeless for a long time. I grew up in Canada, so I thought we had just gone camping. And my parents kept me in the dark, because they were embarrassed. I'd ask, "Dad, are we living below the poverty line?" And he'd say, "No, son. We're rich as long as we have each other. Now get in the Dumpster."

—*Jim Carrey*

Hotels

In hotel rooms I worry. I think, I can't be the only guy who sits on the furniture naked.

—*Jonathan Katz*

Those room-service guys come into your room looking as if they've just been jumped. "Where do you want the food?" Well, there are two flat surfaces; the table or your head.

—*Louie Anderson*

I checked into a hotel the other day, and the woman behind the counter asked, "Do you have a floor preference?" "Yeah, I would like a floor." Apparently, they can suspend you from the ceiling now. She was all impatient. "No, what level?" "Sorry, I'm not that bright. How about . . . beginner?"

—*Paula Poundstone*

What a hotel! The towels were so fluffy I could hardly close my suitcase.

—*Henny Youngman*

I stayed at a Motel 6 the other night. Not only did they leave the light on for me, they also left a half-eaten cheeseburger under the pillowcase and some hair in the shower.

—*Dobie Maxwell*

House

In my house there's this light switch that doesn't do anything. Every so often I would flick it on and off just to check. Yesterday, I got a call from a woman in Germany. She said, "Cut it out."

—*Steven Wright*

Housework

You make the beds, you do the dishes, and six months later you have to start all over again.

—*Joan Rivers*

It is better to light just one candle than to clean the whole apartment.

—*Eileen Courtney*

I bought an electric broom, and my husband said, "Electric brooms are for lazy people. Why don't you use a regular one?" I'm not sure how well my new broom sweeps yet, but it sure works swell to beat a man over the head with.

—*Stephanie Schiern*

I love it when my husband thinks I might leave him. He gets so insecure, he does the dishes. Too bad I have to actually file divorce papers to get him to clean the toilet.

—*Shirley Lipner*

I'm not going to vacuum till Sears makes one you can ride on.

—*Roseanne*

Housework can't kill you, but why take a chance?

—*Phyllis Diller*

Human

The human body is like a condominium apartment. The thing that keeps you from really enjoying it is the maintenance. From showering to open-heart surgery, daily, weekly, monthly, and yearly, we're always doing something to ourselves. If your body was a used car, you wouldn't buy it. "This is one of those Earth models, right? Too much work to keep going. The new ones are nice looking, though."

—*Jerry Seinfeld*

I don't understand the term *human race*. Who are we competing against? And the way things are going, I'm betting on the cockroaches.

—*Joel Warshaw*

Husband

He was cheating on me with his secretary. I found lipstick on his collar, covered with Wite-Out.

—*Wendy Liebman*

He tricked me into marrying him. He told me he was pregnant.

—*Carol Leifer*

My husband said he needed more space. So I locked him outside.

—*Roseanne*

Men are married about six months, and they can't even dress themselves anymore. "Honey, does this tie go with my underwear?"

—*John Mendoza*

I get a lot of ribbing because my husband is so young. While I was smoking my first joint, my husband was only two years old. I got so stoned, I made him drive home.

—*Thyra Lees-Smith*

Ice Cream

I used to live on Ben & Jerry's ice cream. But their flavors are getting a little too radical for me. I draw the line at Chocolate Chicken Liver Chunk.

—*Brock Cohen*

Immigration

Every time an election comes around there's always that same message of love. "You know what's wrong with this country? People from other countries." We're Americans, we all came over on a boat, one way or another. Who is from this country? Technically, only the Indians. Who we graciously let dwell on their native casinos.

—*Greg Proops*

I support making deportations for illegal immigration retroactive, and shipping the Anglos back home.

—*Paul Rodriguez*

Information

I got up one morning and couldn't find my socks, so I called Information. I said, "I can't find my socks." She said, "They're behind the couch." And they were!

—*Steven Wright*

Insects

Some women think that any aerosol can kill a bug. Anything that sprays. "Deodorant! Use that! I've killed bugs with deodorant! Try that." Try killing a monster with deodorant. It's not easy. And all I could find was the roll-on.

—*Ray Romano*

Last weekend my husband and I kept finding all these wasps flying around in our living room, and I would catch them and throw them out the window. I have this idea that it was all the same wasp, he's just into extreme sports.

—*Thyra Lees-Smith*

Insomnia

I'm kinda tired. I was up all night trying to round off infinity. Then I got bored and went out and painted passing lines on curved roads.

—*Steven Wright*

I've read that insomniacs will fall asleep upon hearing five words, "Ladies and Gentlemen . . . Al Gore."

—*Irv Gilman*

Instructions

I once went to Sears to buy a workbench. It came in a big, big box and there was some assembly required. There were instructions, but I didn't need those. Hey, I'm a guy; my balls will tell me how it all fits together.

—*Tim Allen*

Interior Decoration

I put fake brick wallpaper over the real brick walls in my house. So when people come over I can say, "Go ahead, touch it. It feels real."

—*Steven Wright*

Internet

Can anyone tell me why Tampax needs a Web site? "Geez, the cramps are really kicking in. I'd better head over to the maxi-pad chat room to type in 'Kill me.' "

—*Elvira Kurt*

How do you keep kids away from the Internet? Two words: Mandatory Television.

—*Dennis Miller*

Jewelry

My husband gave me a necklace. It's fake. I requested fake. Maybe I'm paranoid, but in this day and age, I don't want something around my neck that's worth more than my head.

—*Rita Rudner*

Job

I tried to get a job at Office Depot and Staples. I didn't need the money. I just wanted to steal from a company that would never run out of office supplies.

—*Wally Wang*

I hate going on job interviews. Like the last one, where they asked me about an eight-month gap in my work history, where I'd suffered from work amnesia. They asked, "What's work amnesia?" I said, "That's when you don't remember what it's like to hold a job."

—*Joel Warshaw*

I used to be a bartender at the Betty Ford Clinic.

—*Steven Wright*

I was a bank teller. That was a great job. I was bringing home $450,000 a week.

—*Joel Lindley*

At Fotomat, what do they do for breaks? Shut the little window, and duck down where no one can see them?

—*Louie Anderson*

How the hell did Marion Barry get his job back? Marion Barry smoked crack and got his job back as mayor. If you get caught smoking crack at McDonald's you're not going to get your job back. They can't trust you around the Happy Meals. They'll send your ass to Hardee's.

—*Chris Rock*

Foreigners do not come to this country and take our jobs. Face it, you don't want to be a busboy, or a maid, or the roadside Linus Pauling hawking citrus on a traffic island.

—*Dennis Miller*

Last year I left my job to stay home with my kids. One nice thing about it is, I'm my own boss. So I declared Real Casual Fridays. I don't get out of bed.

—*Eileen Courtney*

Keys

The other night I came home late and tried to unlock my house with my car keys. I started the house up. So, I drove it around for a while. I was speeding, and a cop pulled me over. He asked where I lived. I said, "Right here, Officer." Later, I parked it on the freeway, got out, and yelled at all the cars, "Get out of my driveway!"

—*Steven Wright*

Kids

My girlfriend Holly and I went to visit a friend who has two children. Afterward all Holly could talk about was how cute the kids were. That's pretty scary to a single guy. The only time scarier was when she was shaking the stick from the pregnancy kit, and I was yelling like I was at the roulette table in Vegas, "Come on blue! Come on blue!"

—*Joel Warshaw*

My mother used to say to us kids, "What did I do to deserve you monsters?" And I thought, "Mom, boys don't come from cauliflowers, and girls from roses. Wake up, you just had sex with the wrong guy."

—*Jim Rez*

I love my kids, but I need something more. Like, perhaps, a life.

—*Roseanne*

When you're a parent you give up your freedom. You sleep according to someone else's schedule, you eat according to someone else's schedule. It's like being in jail, but you really love the warden.

—*Lew Schneider*

Everyone should have kids. They are the greatest joy in the world. But they are also terrorists. You'll realize this as soon as they're born, and they start using sleep deprivation to break you.

—*Ray Romano*

People have always told me that I'd learn more from my kids than they'd learn from me. I believe that. I've learned that, as a parent, when you have sex your body emits a hormone that drifts down the hall into your child's room and makes them want a drink of water.

—*Jeff Foxworthy*

I like my kids a lot, but it's like a rodeo clown car pulled up and fifteen of them got out and they're running around. It's like they're monkeys on acid and they're hanging on lamps and lights and the ceiling. Get down!

—*Denis Leary*

Kids, your parents used to be cool. There's a country music song title that always makes me laugh, "You're the Reason Our Kids Are Ugly." Someday I'm gonna record my song to my kids, "You're the Reason I'm Not Cool Anymore."

—*Sinbad*

The real menace in dealing with a five-year-old is that in no time at all you begin to sound like a five-year-old.

—*Jean Kerr*

When you're a kid you can be friends with anybody. If someone is in front of my house right now, that's my friend. "Are you a grown-up? No? Come in and jump on my bed!" And if you have anything in common, "You like cherry soda, I like cherry soda! We'll be best friends!"

—*Jerry Seinfeld*

I had to go to fat camp every summer. I hated it. Too many rules. Like only three meals a day. One kid to a cabin. Two kids in the lake. A sign that warned, "Don't feed the children."

—*Louie Anderson*

If I ever had twins, I'd use one for parts.

—*Steven Wright*

I have two kids, and over the years I've developed a really relaxed attitude about the whole child-rearing thing. I don't cry over spilt milk. Spilt vodka, that's another story.

—*Daryl Hogue*

Adults are always asking little kids what they want to be when they grow up, 'cause they're looking for ideas.

—*Paula Poundstone*

Kids are cute, but they're so rude. I was taking a shower, when my daughter came in and said, "Gosh, Mom. I hope when I grow up my breasts are nice and long like yours."

—*Roseanne*

Living with my daughters is like driving on the freeway. At first I'm optimistic, but gradually I'll just settle for no bloodshed.

—*Gloria Brinkworth*

As a kid, I used to wander around in the woods. Because my parents had put me there.

—*Ellen DeGeneres*

At the mall I saw a kid on a leash. And I think if I ever have a kid, it's gonna be cordless.

—*Wendy Liebman*

Eight kids in my family. You kind of get lost in the shuffle. We had to wear a name tag to Thanksgiving dinner.

—*Brian Regan*

When I was a kid I got no respect. I had no friends. I remember the seesaw. I had to keep runnin' from one end to the other.

—*Rodney Dangerfield*

I was a gay kid. My parents said, "We never suspected." Give me a break. They gave me a chemistry set, and I used it to make my own line of skin-care products.

—*Bob Smith*

One day I want to have kids, I'm just not ready yet. But I love to play with kids. And the best thing about playing with someone else's child is, they're not yours, so you can break them.

—*Joel Warshaw*

The best way to keep children at home is to make the home atmosphere pleasant, and let the air out of their tires.

—*Dorothy Parker*

Knowledge

There's useless stuff in my brain. I don't know why I know it. It's never gonna be a category on *Jeopardy!* "Yeah, Alex, I'll take Useless Shit for five hundred, please." "The answer is . . . George Glass." *Ding*! "Who was Jan's imaginary boyfriend?"

—*Rosie O'Donnell*

Law

The Miranda rights, as I see them: You have the right to remain silent, and to wear bananas on your head.

—*Joy Behar*

I think the Brady Bill is working. I was in New York and I heard a guy say, "Give me your wallet, or I'll blow your brains out in five business days."

—*Jonathan Katz*

Lawyer

A lawyer is basically the person who knows the rules of the country. We're all throwing the dice, playing the game, moving our pieces around the board. But if there's a problem, the lawyer is the only person who has read the inside of the top of the box.

—*Jerry Seinfeld*

Lazy

I'm the laziest person. I know I'm not supposed to admit that because—wooo, the work ethic! We lazy slobs get such a bad rap, but you people should be thanking us. Because if it weren't for us lazy bastards, you guys wouldn't have gotten into college.

—*Ann Oelschlager*

Scientists at the University of Glasgow in Scotland believe there may be a gene for laziness. People who suspect they have inherited this gene can perform a simple test at home: Look in the mirror and see if you've got a big, fat ass.

—*Craig Kilborn*

Leather

A lady came up to me on the street and pointed at my suede jacket. "You know a cow was murdered for that jacket?" she sneered. I replied in a psychotic tone, "I didn't know there were any witnesses. Now I'll have to kill you, too."

—*Jake Johannsen*

Lesbian

My favorite, the classic parental guilt trip, "Is this the way it's going to be for you? One woman after another, for the rest of your life?" God, I hope so.

—*Elvira Kurt*

It's not that I don't like penises. I just don't like them on men.

—*Lea DeLaria*

Heterosexuals are rude sometimes, get right in your face and ask you rude questions: "What do you lesbians do in bed?" Well, it's a lot like heterosexual sex. Only one of us doesn't have to fake an orgasm.

—*Suzanne Westenhoefer*

Letter

Friends write me letters, run out of room on the front, and write "over" on the bottom. Like I'm that much of a moron. Because if it wasn't there, I'd get to the bottom of the page: "And so Kathy and I went shopping and we . . ." "That's the craziest thing! I don't know why she would just end it that way."

—*Ellen DeGeneres*

Library

The library gives you any book you want and says, "Please just bring it back when you're done." Like that pathetic kid who would let you borrow any of his stuff, if you would just be his friend. Everybody bullies the library a little, because it's a government-funded pathetic friend. "Maybe I'll bring it back on time, maybe I'll bring it late. What you gonna do, charge me a nickel? I'm *soo* scared."

—*Jerry Seinfeld*

Life

The best things in life really are free. So, how many kittens do you want?

—*Nancy Jo Perdue*

In first grade my teacher asked what I expected of life. I said, "You color for a while, and then you die."

—*Jeffrey Essmann*

My life hasn't gone the way I thought it would. I'm in therapy now and I'm trying to find the exact moment that things went wrong. I've narrowed it down to conception.

—*Joel Warshaw*

Life is anything that dies when you stomp on it.

—*Dave Barry*

Life isn't fair. My husband's birthday is October 9. When it falls on a Monday, it's Columbus Day, a holiday. My birthday is April 17. When it falls on Monday, it's tax day. My thirtieth birthday fell on Monday, it was tax day, raining, and I was pregnant. If you throw in a dog and a pickup truck, you've got all the makings of a country song.

—*Shannon Ireland*

The cost of living is going up, and the chance of living is going down.

—*Flip Wilson*

Life is something that happens when you can't get to sleep.

—*Fran Lebowitz*

I could be bitter about my life, but I'm not. It's not what happens to you, it's how you choose to deal with it. I find Prozac or a killing spree works best. If you see me on *Cops*, you'll know the Prozac didn't work.

—*Daryl Hogue*

Limousine

You know what I never get about the limo? The tinted windows. Nobody cares who is in the limo. You see a limousine go by, you know it's either a rich guy or fifty prom kids with $1.75 each.

—*Jerry Seinfeld*

Living Room

My idea of the perfect living room would be the bridge on the starship *Enterprise*. Big chair, nice screen, remote control. *Star Trek* was the ultimate male fantasy: Hurtling through space in your living room, watching TV. That's why the aliens were always dropping in, Kirk had the big screen.

—*Jerry Seinfeld*

Living Will

People who do not want to be resuscitated now have the option to wear a bracelet that says DO NOT RESUSCITATE. To me this sounds like a great gift for someone you hate. What if you put the wrong bracelet on one night? You're out having dinner, you pass out, and twenty minutes later you're in the morgue. And all you wanted to do was accessorize.

—*Joy Behar*

Love

What is love? An extension of like. What is lust? An extension.

—*Rodney Dangerfield*

A guy knows he's in love when he loses interest in his car for a couple days.

—*Tim Allen*

There is no love at first sight. And what do you mean by it exactly? You saw a woman putting gas in her car and you knew you were in love? Maybe it was the gas fumes, fool.

—*Sinbad*

Before I met my husband I'd never fallen in love, though I've stepped in it a few times.

—*Rita Rudner*

Luck

I busted a mirror and got seven years bad luck. But my lawyer thinks he can get me five.

—*Steven Wright*

Magazine

There's very little advice in men's magazines, because men don't think there's a lot they don't know. Women want to learn. Men think, "I know what I'm doing, just show me somebody naked."

—*Jerry Seinfeld*

This one girl I saw in *Playboy* was so amazing. I don't think she had silicone, I think she had helium. She was so big I couldn't keep the magazine closed.

—*Rita Rudner*

I don't understand the *Sports Illustrated* swimsuit issue. Bikini models in a magazine about sports? That'll make sense the day I see Dick Butkus in the Victoria's Secret catalog.

—*Sheila Wenz*

Marriage

My mother always said, "Don't marry for money. Divorce for money."

—*Wendy Liebman*

My husband and I didn't sign a prenuptial agreement. We signed a mutual suicide pact.

—*Roseanne*

That married couples can live together day after day is a miracle that the Vatican has overlooked.

—*Bill Cosby*

Marriage is the roughest thing in the world. Nelson Mandela endured twenty-seven years in a South African prison. But once he got out, it only took two years before his marriage busted his ass.

—*Chris Rock*

The whole idea of marriage is so repulsive. Life is a grim sludge-trek toward death. If you're married, you have to make that sludge-trek with someone going, "C'mon, would you hurry up already?"

—*Patton Oswalt*

Till death do you part, that's biblical. But they didn't live long in those days, they had good plagues. Soon as that guy got on your nerves, here come some locusts to eat his ass. Now we got antibiotics, personal trainers, and tofu. We hang around forever. You end up just looking at each other, "I see you got up today. You should start smoking."

—*Wanda Sykes-Hall*

Being married is like eating at Denny's. As long as your expectations aren't too high, you may enjoy the Grand Slam breakfast.

—*Jeff Stilson*

I love being married. It's so great to find that one special person you want to annoy for the rest of your life.

—*Rita Rudner*

I was married for a short time. Just long enough to realize all those comedians weren't joking.

—*Daniel Lybra*

My wife would not live with me before we were married. Now that we've been together for a while, I'm trying to convince her to get her own place again.

—*Jeff Jena*

Before I got married, my wife told me, "Don't talk about sex until we get married." We got married and she said, "Now you can talk about it all you want."

—*Rodney Dangerfield*

You know you're married when you're lying in bed with somebody and you suddenly think, "Uh oh, I've got to go home, my wife's waiting on me."

—*Jeff Foxworthy*

According to *Psychology Today,* to keep your sex life active as a married couple, you should engage in role playing. This works. Once a month my wife and I check into a cheap motel, and she pretends to be a hooker while I pretend to be a TV evangelist.

—*Wally Wang*

I think the bottom-line difference between being single and being married is this: When you're single you're as happy as you are. When you're married, you can only be as happy as the least happy person in the apartment.

—*Tom Hertz*

In Hollywood a marriage is a success if it outlasts milk.

—*Rita Rudner*

The beauty part is, in any couple only one person has to be sane at a time. You talk them out of their tree, so they can be coherent enough to talk you out of your tree. All the time you spend trying to understand the other person isn't even for their sake. You just want to make sure they're ready to handle your next psychotic episode.

—*Paul Reiser*

When you're newly married, you fight over three things; money, sex, and in-laws. After twenty-one years, you stop fighting. You realize you'll never have the first two, and you'll always have the last one.

—*Shannon Ireland*

I've been married for forty-three years, and it ain't easy. By way of comparison, forty-three years is longer than most murderers spend in jail.

—*Irv Gilman*

Martial Arts

I'm only 5'2", and so I took tae kwon do lessons for a couple years. I loved it, but we were always paired up to fight with someone our own size. So now I can kick any twelve-year-old's butt on the planet.

—*Daryl Hogue*

Medication

If you took NyQuil and No-Doz at the same time, would you dream you couldn't sleep?

—*Carrot Top*

A new study shows that estrogen appears to help protect women's memories from decline due to aging. After being given estrogen, researchers found that women once again were able to bring up things their husbands did years ago and throw it back in their faces.

—*Johnny Robish*

Medicine

The only difference between alternative medicine and an HMO is that more doctors believe HMOs don't work.

—*Wally Wang*

The *Journal of the American Medical Association* says that a third of all drug complications in hospitals are due to errors. The other two-thirds were intentional, or recreational.

—*Johnny Robish*

I'm very resourceful. The other day, this man passed out from a heart attack. So I hooked up my jumper cables and turned on the engine. I didn't save his life, but I cloned my Hyundai.

—*Fran Chernowsky*

I love New York City emergency rooms. "My friend here accidentally stabbed himself in the back, twenty-nine times. Go figure. He was loading his knife, and it went off."

—*Billy Crystal*

One of the most difficult things to contend with in a hospital is the assumption on the part of the staff that because you have lost your gallbladder you have also lost your mind.

—*Jean Kerr*

Mammogram. You ever get one of those things? They put your breast in a vise and take it hostage. Start cranking it shut, like you have the secret rocket formula. You don't think it's ever going to get back into its natural shape again, you'll be rolling it up to get it back in the bra. Put a little ham key on the end of it.

—*Margaret Smith*

I don't get along with nurses. They're vicious to women. When my friend Trudy was in labor, the nurse looked down at her and said, "Still think blondes have more fun?"

—*Joan Rivers*

Japan has done their first organ transplant. Because they've had taboos in Japan about cutting up corpses, cultural taboos, but they've apparently overcome that. And the great thing about the Japanese transplant is they do it right there at your table.

—*Bill Maher*

I went to Gus's artificial organ and taco stand. I said, "Give me a bladder, *por favor*." The guy said, "Is that to go?" Well, what else would I want it for?

—*Emo Philips*

When I was a kid I was poor. I never got an X ray. My old man would hold me up to the light.

—*Rodney Dangerfield*

Meditation

My son has taken up meditation. At least it's better than sitting doing nothing.

—*Max Kauffman*

Men

I know what men want. Men want to be really, really close to someone who will leave them alone.

—*Elayne Boosler*

My mom said the only reason men are alive is for lawn care and vehicle maintenance.

—*Tim Allen*

What do men do normally? Endlessly congratulate each other, and wander around in small groups looking for something to break.

—*Robin Williams*

A guy with a little bit of a potbelly, it says something about the guy: he's relaxed about the fat slob he's become. And women like that.

—*Jonathan Katz*

Honking the horn at a woman amazes me. What's she supposed to do? Kick off the heels, start running after, hang on to the bumper? "It's a good thing you honked, or I wouldn't have known how you felt."

—*Jerry Seinfeld*

I'm so sick of men saying that women have all the power, because men are slaves to their penis. What you mean is that the one percent of women who look like *Playboy* centerfolds can get you to do anything—and the other 99 percent of us can't get a tire changed at rush hour. "Excuse me, sir! Oh, I guess he's gotta go home to log on at the Pamela Anderson Web site."

—*Ann Oelschlager*

Women think men are led around by our penises. It points us in a direction, I'll give you that. But we're adult enough to make a decision whether to follow it. Granted, I put my back out trying to reel it back in.

—*Garry Shandling*

I can't stand macho men who have to run everything. Three times last week my boyfriend asked me if I checked the oil in my car. Three times last week while we were having sex, he said, "Honey, have you checked your oil?" I said, "You're the one with the dipstick, you do it!"

—*Tamara Kastle*

God gave us a penis and a brain, but not enough blood to use both at the same time.

—*Robin Williams*

Men are pigs. Too bad we own everything.

—Tim Allen

Watch the way men express physical intimacy. We don't just hug and hold. What we do is hug with one arm, and with the other we pat on the back. That's basically saying, "Yeah, I'm hugging you, but I'm also hitting ya!"

—Lew Schneider

Men do not like to admit to even momentary imperfection. My husband forgot the code to turn off the alarm. When the police came, he wouldn't admit he'd forgotten the code. He turned himself in.

—Rita Rudner

The younger men, all right! They still come too quick and go to sleep right after, but they can do it every goddamn night.

—Roseanne

Women get their heart broke, they cry. Men don't do that. Men hold it in like it don't hurt. They walk around and get hit by trucks. "Didn't he see that truck?" "Man, he wouldn't have seen a 747. His heart was broke."

—Richard Pryor

Men look at women the way men look at cars. Everyone looks at Ferraris. Now and then we like a pickup truck. And we all end up with a station wagon.

—*Tim Allen*

When are women going to realize that men like to look at other women? It doesn't mean we love them any less. Last Saturday night I took my girlfriend to this place where there were a lot of beautiful women, so naturally I was looking around. But all night she kept nagging me, "Can we please get out of this strip club?"

—*Joel Warshaw*

A medical study reports that men who wear gold wedding bands suffer less pain from arthritis in their hands. It's not from the gold, it's from constantly working their fingers taking the ring off when a girl walks by.

—*Jay Leno*

They say you can compare a man's shoe size to his manhood. So that's why I keep my skis on everywhere I go.

—*Garry Shandling*

Military

I was serving my country. It was either that or six months.

—*Richard Pryor*

The whole idea of the military strikes me as completely absurd. What sense does it make to go off somewhere thousands of miles away to a scorching desert, to kill a lot of people who have never done anything to me, when I can sit in the air-conditioned comfort of my own home and take out a few people who really matter?

—*E. L. Greggory*

Ban gays and lesbians in the military? Are you kidding? If you took all the lesbians out of the WACs, you'd be left with four typists.

—*Robin Tyler*

If they don't want lesbians in the military, we should get out. Because someday the USA will go to war again, and all the straight people will go die for our rights, and we'll get to hang out here. "Bye. You be careful. Don't worry, we'll take care of your wives."

—*Suzanne Westenhoefer*

The Swiss have an interesting army. Five hundred years without a war. Pretty lucky for them. Ever see that little Swiss Army knife they have to fight with? Not much of a weapon there. Corkscrews. Bottle openers. "Back off, I've got toe clippers."

—*Jerry Seinfeld*

We have women in the military, but they don't put us in the front lines. They don't know if we can kill. I think we can. All the general has to do is walk over to the women and say, "You see the enemy over there? They say you look fat in those uniforms."

—*Elayne Boosler*

The Pentagon wants the Navy to start putting women on their submarines. The Navy is trying to resist. But the Pentagon wants to promote diversity, and also give the gay guys someone to dish with.

—*Bill Maher*

Vietnam vets, I have a lot of empathy for them. They had to go to a horrible place and perform a hideous job for people who didn't even appreciate it. I know what that's like, I used to be a waitress at Denny's.

—*Roseanne*

A scientist at a university in England says that within five years robots could fight wars, rather than humans. There are two advantages of an all-robot army. First, it would greatly decrease the incidence of human casualties. Second: way fewer incidents of sexual harassment.

—Craig Kilborn

Militias

Militias are a bunch of crazy white dudes who are mad at the government. But the government of this country was constructed for white men, by white men. Wasn't nobody else covered in the Constitution. No black people, no Indians, no Jews, no women. We might have been there when they was writing the Constitution, but y'all had us serving the tea. Didn't ask us what it should say.

—D. L. Hughley

Models

Why do models look so mean? I went to a fashion show, the model's wearing ten thousand dollars' worth of stuff, fifteen-thousand-dollar shoes, and mad! You know why they're mad? 'Cause they're hungry, that's why.

—Mark Curry

Money

I hate pennies, I can never seem to spend them. I must have five dollars' worth at the bottom of my purse. In my case, a penny saved isn't a penny earned, it's a two-hundred-dollar trip to the chiropractor.

—*Stephanie Schiern*

Lately, I've really been enjoying how fast and easy banking through an automated system can be. I walk up to the machine, I stick in my card, and I get a receipt. The downside is, it feels like I'm having sex with my ex-girlfriend.

—*Joel Warshaw*

I used one of those change machines. I put a dollar in, got four quarters back. I was thinking, the owner of this machine at the end of each day must be like, "I broke even, again? I need more machines."

—*Tom Hertz*

I'm not very good at saving money. My parents say, "A penny saved is a penny earned." But if that's true, then my vacuum is the World Bank.

—*Lesley Wake*

I put a dollar in a change machine. Nothing changed.

—*George Carlin*

I don't own real estate, but I have some really nice sweaters.

—*Carrie Snow*

My standard of living keeps going down since divorce, and my ex-husband's keeps going up. He was offered something called the Titanium card, that's even better than Platinum. Based on my credit, Citibank offered me the Plywood card.

—*Maura Kennedy*

It was tough asking thrifty parents for money. You've got to beg fathers: "Dad, can I have a dollar?" "What happened to the dollar I gave you last year?"

—*Sinbad*

Someday I want to be rich. Some people get so rich they lose all respect for humanity. That's how rich I want to be.

—*Rita Rudner*

I never had a penny to my name. So I changed my name.

—*Henny Youngman*

Mother

My mom breast-fed me. It was only 2 percent.

—*Wendy Liebman*

I love being a mom. My four-year-old son tells me how pretty I am, that he loves me and wants to marry me. I love him, too, but I don't think he could support me in the style to which I'm accustomed. Not as a Power Ranger, anyway.

—*Liz Sells*

You want to hear the childhood daredevil stories my mother tells company? "Once a glass broke on the kitchen floor, not one week later my daughter was in there without her shoes on." I broke a glass in 1954, they sold the house in 1985, my mother warned the new owners, "I think I got all the big pieces, but there could be slivers."

—*Elayne Boosler*

There's an old saying, "Neurotics build castles in the air, and psychotics live in them." My mother cleans them.

—*Rita Rudner*

My mother was eighty-eight years old. She never used glasses. Drank right out of the bottle!

—*Henny Youngman*

I was raised in Phoenix by very conservative parents. My mother still calls herself Mrs. Donald Williams. I try to picture her at parties, "Hi, my name is Mrs. Donald Williams. But you can call me Don."

—*Danny Williams*

My mom taught me everything I needed to know. Don't talk to strangers, don't pay retail, and the size of your hair should always match the size of your ass.

—*Stephanie Schiern*

My mom is very possessive. She calls me up and says, "You weren't home last night. Is something going on?" I said, "Yeah, Mom. I'm cheating on you with another mother."

—*Heidi Joyce*

God bless my mom, she had reverse Alzheimer's. Towards the end she remembered everything, and she was pissed.

—*S. Rachel Lovey*

Motivation

Motivational tapes and books. Either you want to do something or you don't, it's a fairly simple thing. Besides, if you were motivated enough to go to the store to buy a motivation book, doesn't that prove you're motivated? Put it back, tell the clerk, "Screw you, I'm motivated," and go home.

—George Carlin

Movies

Universal had to push back the date of their Thanksgiving release of the sequel to the pig movie *Babe*. Production was thrown off schedule when the caterers made a terrible, terrible mistake.

—Colin Quinn

The Blair Witch Project. A shaky, handheld home movie about homely teens who would still be alive today if only they'd gotten summer jobs at Spencer Gifts.

—Frank DeCaro

Why is it that the soda costs more than the tickets? They serve you a cup of Coke so large, Ted Kennedy could drop an Oldsmobile into it. Which means halfway through the movie you're so bloated you have to step outside for twenty minutes of dialysis.

—Dennis Miller

The big hot movie is *The Blair Witch Project*. Yeah, I saw it, but I didn't get it. Maybe because that's how my last family camping trip ended.

—*Joel Warshaw*

I liked *Free Willy,* but they had *Free Willy 2, Free Willy Again*. He keeps getting caught, you'd think he'd learn. "I let you go once, I can't be doing this all the time. You're hard to sneak."

—*John Pinette*

The Mod Squad is now on video. About an African-American man, a rich kid, and a woman who come together to fight crime. I understand Dennis Rodman was up for all three parts.

—*Jay Leno*

In scary movies, people always get bitten in the neck. To me, that means they don't even try to run. If a vampire gets close to me, I'm off and running away! When they find my body, the police will say, "Call *The X-Files*. This man has two holes in his butt, and no blood in his body."

—*Sinbad*

Some people you can't shush in a movie theater. They're talking and talking, everyone around them is shushing them, and they won't shush. No one can shush them. They're the unshushables.

—*Jerry Seinfeld*

I hate renting at Blockbuster, because I'm a single guy, and don't feel comfortable with that five-day commitment. That's waaay too long. Renting a video should be like a one-night stand. You pick it up, take it home to a darkened room, and the next morning, you return it to where you found it.

—*Joel Warshaw*

Moving

When you're moving your whole world becomes finding boxes. You become obsessed. You could be at a funeral, everyone's crying, you're looking at the casket. "That's a nice box. It even has handles on it."

—*Jerry Seinfeld*

I'm moving to Mars next week. So, if you have any boxes . . .

—*Steven Wright*

Music

I take music pretty seriously. This scar on my wrist, do you know what that's from? I heard the Bee Gees were getting back together again.

—*Denis Leary*

I had a dream I was trapped in an elevator with Michael Bolton, Kenny G, and Yanni. And I had a gun with only one bullet.

—*Dave Attell*

I don't understand the importance of the conductor. What the hell is this guy doing? Do you really need somebody waving a stick in front of your face to play the violin?

—*Jerry Seinfeld*

You might be a country music fan—if you want to write country music, but you can't think of any clean words that rhyme with *truck*.

—*Brian Koffman*

House music, "You've got to work it! You've got to push it!" I don't gotta do anything. I don't like being ordered around by my music. Take it down a notch.

—*Dave Attell*

We don't have no real deep love songs no more, just songs that mean a lot in the ghetto, " 'Cause I'm Your Daddy, You Can Page Me Anytime."

—*Cedric the Entertainer*

Marilyn Manson was on tour with Courtney Love and it didn't work out. Apparently, Courtney was scaring off all the Satan worshipers.

—*Bill Maher*

Somebody just gave me a shower radio. Thanks a lot. Do you really want music in the shower? I guess there's no better place to dance than a slick surface next to a glass door.

—*Jerry Seinfeld*

White people do not come up with the good music. White people invented polka, and Gregorian chants, and Country. White people invented Swiss clock dancing. "Whoo, Heidi, little goat girl, you are kickin' the jam!" Leave white people isolated for a thousand years, and their contribution is *Riverdance*: "I can't move my hips, I can't move my head. But below the ankles, I'm a rockin' bag of Gaelic sex!"

—*Greg Proops*

I was listening to some rap music this afternoon. Not that I had a choice, it was coming out of a Jeep four miles away.

—*Nick Capallo*

Yo. Yo. Yo. Yo. Yo . . . Yo. I can't seem to get the new Lauryn Hill song out of my head.

—*Brock Cohen*

Neighbor

What do you do when a neighbor is making a lot of noise at three o'clock in the morning? How can you knock on someone's door and ask them to keep it down, if it alters your whole self-image? What am I, Fred Mertz? Am I a shusher? I used to be a shushee.

—*Jerry Seinfeld*

Neighborhood

I tell ya, I come from a tough neighborhood. Why, just last week some guy pulled a knife on me. I could see it wasn't a real professional job. There was butter on it.

—*Rodney Dangerfield*

My mother's house, exposed bricks and nerves. She lives in a predominantly anxious part of town.

—*Richard Lewis*

I grew up in the suburbs in a neighborhood that was not very tough at all. Even our school bully was only passively aggressive. He wouldn't take your lunch, he'd just say, "You're going to eat all that?"

—*Brian Kiley*

Nephew

My nephews love spending time with me, because I let them do anything they want. They're not my kids. Only thing I have to do is keep them alive, that's all. "Ice cream all day? Sure, I don't have to cook, just scoop. Eat up, I don't pay your dental bills."

—*Wanda Sykes-Hall*

News

There's a lot of violence in the media. In reporting violent crime the local news comports itself with all the dignity of Moe, Larry, and Shemp locked in a haunted house.

—*Dennis Miller*

Former CNN reporter Peter Arnett is planning to write a history of the Cable News Network. The first chapter of the book is titled, "Ted Turner's Dad Dies, and Ted Inherits a Lot of Money."

—*Craig Kilborn*

You can tell it's a slow news week when you see articles like "Did Comets Kill the Dinosaurs?" Here's a hot topic. Maybe comets killed the dinosaurs, maybe they tripped and fell. We'll never know. We couldn't solve the Kennedy assassination, we had films of that. Good luck with the stegosaurus.

—*Jerry Seinfeld*

Zillionaire Microsoft Chairman Bill Gates announced a plan to give one billion dollars to fund scholarships for minority students. The donation comes with some strings attached. The NAACP must now be renamed MSNAACP.

—*Craig Kilborn*

The prosecutor trying to get Dr. Kevorkian said, "You gotta convict this man because his next victim may be an eighteen-year-old girl who wants to die because she has boyfriend troubles." But Dr. Kevorkian said he would never do that. First of all, it's no fun killing anyone whose last words are "Yeah, *whatever.*"

—*Bill Maher*

Dr. Kevorkian was sentenced to ten to twenty-five years in prison for second-degree murder. By the time he gets out, everyone he wanted to kill will already be dead.

—*Jay Leno*

Angry New Hampshire taxpayers reenacted the Boston Tea Party by dumping fifty boxes of tax bills into Portsmouth harbor. Hey, knock it off. Thousands of homeless people drink out of that harbor every night.

—*Craig Kilborn*

This guy trying to set some kind of stupid record drove his lawn mower fifty-one hundred miles across country. Do you know who I feel sorry for? The guy walking behind him with the edger.

—*Jay Leno*

Justice William Rehnquist of the Supreme Court recently led a judicial conference in a rousing rendition of "Dixie." And people have said this old slavery song is inappropriate for a Chief Justice to sing. It especially offended Clarence Thomas, who said, "If he's going to sing 'Dixie,' I'm going to sing my favorites, the theme songs from *Hair* and *Shaft*."

—*Bill Maher*

The emotional, psychological, and mental evaluation test-score results on the Unabomber came back. Monday he starts at the post office.

—*David Brenner*

UN inspectors have gone back to Iraq, but Saddam still won't let them near anyplace where he has something to hide. So the inspectors haven't found any biological, chemical, or nuclear weapons. The most they've done is close down a coffee shop in Baghdad, because the fry cook wasn't wearing a hair net.

—*Bill Maher*

Indonesian officials have accepted the presence of UN peacekeepers to help control rioting that gripped the country. The bloodshed began after East Timor rappers dissed West Timor rappers, setting off a bicoastal rap war.

—*Craig Kilborn*

Newspaper

Sunday paper is the worst. You want to relax. "Oh, by the way, here's a thousand pages of information you had no idea about." How can they tell you everything they know every single day of the week, and then have this much left over on Sunday, when nothing's going on?

—*Jerry Seinfeld*

Nostalgia

People say, "It's not like the good old days." When were these good old days? In 1900 your doctor was also your barber. "Uh, take a little off the sides when you take out my spleen."

—*Joe Ditzel*

Olympics

So many events in the Olympics, I don't understand their connection to reality. Like in the Winter Olympics, the biathlon that combines cross-country skiing with shooting a gun. How many Alpine snipers are into this? To me it's like combining swimming with strangling a guy.

—*Jerry Seinfeld*

The triathlons, they bike and then they swim. Why? Either these people don't have jobs, or they have jobs that are incredibly difficult to get to.

—*Rita Rudner*

I got to go to the Fat Olympics. I won the Hula Hoop contest. I'm still wearing it. The pole vault? I drove that sucker into the ground. I did a good deed, too. I straightened out the uneven bars. And the broad jump? I killed her.

—*Louie Anderson*

Optimism

Things could be much worse. I could be one of my creditors.

—*Henny Youngman*

Painkillers

The pain-relieving ingredient, there's always got to be a lot of that. Nobody wants anything less than extra strength. "Give me the maximum allowable human dosage. Figure out what will kill me, and then back it off a little bit."

—Jerry Seinfeld

Can you imagine what a nightmare it must have been before they invented painkillers? What did they do, have a guy bite a bullet? They could have done better than that. Bring in a big-breasted woman. That would distract any man. Stick a knife through their arm, they see those big breasts, they don't feel a thing.

—Joy Behar

Paint

I went to the hardware store and bought some used paint. It was in the shape of a house.

—Steven Wright

Painting

I've been doing a lot of abstract painting lately, extremely abstract. No brush, no paint, no canvas, I just think about it.

—Steven Wright

Paperweight

There's nothing compares to the paperweight as a bad gift. And where are these people working that their papers are just blowing right off their desks? Is their office screwed to the back of a flatbed truck going down the highway? Are they typing up in the crow's nest of a clipper ship?

—Jerry Seinfeld

Parents

You don't know what love is until you become a parent. You don't know what love is until you fish a turd out of the bathtub for someone.

—Margaret Smith

Raising a child may be a labor of love, but nonetheless, it is a job. Usually a fun job. But sometimes so frustrating, menial, and dull, it makes working the corn dog concession in the Ringworm Brothers Carnival seem like a stint in the double-O sector of Her Majesty's Secret Service.

—*Dennis Miller*

Fortunately, my parents were intelligent, enlightened people. They accepted me for what I was, a punishment from God.

—*David Steinberg*

I've noticed that one thing about parents is that no matter what stage your child is in, the parents who have older children always tell you the next stage is worse.

—*Dave Barry*

Parents are not quite interested in justice, they are interested in quiet.

—*Bill Cosby*

I think my parents rushed me toward adulthood, they gave me an adult name. My name is Lew and my younger brother's name is Sam. Those aren't kids, that's a retail outlet. Lew and Sam, Discount Carpeting, Come On In.

—*Lew Schneider*

My parents actually met in junior high school. I guess they figured: What the heck, once you've seen someone in junior high, you've pretty much seen them at their worst.

—*Norman K.*

Parents can overestimate their kid's abilities. At my last parent-teacher conference, a father said, "My son shouldn't have gotten a fifty. He's got a photographic memory." If that kid has a photographic memory, somebody exposed the film. At Kmart, he'd get half his money back.

—*Lesley Wake*

You don't ever really want to visualize your parents having sex. It's very uncomfortable. Sex is a great thing and all. But you don't want to think that your whole life began because somebody had a little too much wine with dinner.

—*Jerry Seinfeld*

My parents are traveling in the Middle East. Tension broke out in Jerusalem today because Leo wouldn't ask for directions.

—*Cathy Ladman*

I took my parents back to the airport today. They leave tomorrow.

—*Margaret Smith*

My parents are always calling me out in California. To find out what time it is. "What time is it out there?" "It's three hours' difference, Mom. Work it out on paper."

—*Kevin Meaney*

Every Sunday I talk to my parents in Arizona. They live in a retirement community, which is basically a minimum-security prison with a golf course.

—*Joel Warshaw*

My parents' dream was for me to have everything they didn't. And thanks to ozone holes, fear of AIDS, and no health insurance, their dream has come true.

—*Brad Slaight*

There's a new book, *Parents Don't Matter,* which says that growing up, your peer group affects you more than your parents. I'm not sure I believe that. It's much easier to blame your parents. I still have their phone number.

—*Norman K.*

If your parents never had children, chances are you won't either.

—*Dick Cavett*

Pessimism

I guess I just prefer to see the dark side of things. The glass is always half empty. And cracked. And I just cut my lip on it. And chipped a tooth.

—*Janeane Garofalo*

Some mornings, it's just not worth chewing through the leather straps.

—*Emo Philips*

Pets

My roommate got a pet elephant. Then it got lost. It's in the apartment somewhere.

—*Steven Wright*

Pharmacist

Why does that pharmacist have to be two and a half feet higher than everybody else? Who the hell is this guy? "I'm working with pills up here. I'm taking them from this big bottle, and I'm going to put them into a little bottle. I can't be down on the floor with you people."

—*Jerry Seinfeld*

Philosophy

I'm not a fatalist. But even if I were, what could I do about it?

—*Emo Philips*

What if everything is an illusion and nothing exists? In that case, I definitely overpaid for my carpet.

—*Woody Allen*

Photographs

I have some very rare photographs. One is of Houdini locking his keys in his car.

—*Steven Wright*

Physique

You women ever talk about men's bodies like they're meat? I know you do, every time you're with your girlfriends, "Look at that baby. That's USDA Choice Prime Cut." My body is the part they make hot dogs out of. I have a lips and a hooves kind of body.

—*Drew Carey*

I have flabby thighs, but fortunately my stomach covers them.

—*Joan Rivers*

I don't have an hourglass figure. I have an hour and half. I have a little too much time on my ass.

—*Wendy Liebman*

I took a physical for some life insurance. All they would give me was fire and theft.

—*Henny Youngman*

It sucks being a small guy, because I can't fight anyone. My neighbor keeps his music really loud, so I had to go upstairs, be like, "Excuse me, could you please turn your music down?" "Are you a moron?" " . . . Yeah." I've often thought about just jumping on him when he turns around, but then he'd be like, "Do you want a piggyback ride?"

—*Mitch Fatel*

Martin Luther King was a little guy. Malcolm X was a big guy. The little guy talked about us all getting along. The big guy talked about whupping ass. Little guys only fight when there's no other choice. I know MLK was a devout Christian and humanitarian, but if he was four or five inches taller, his message might have been totally different. And we might be dead right now.

—*Chris Rock*

Bad body image for women is out of control. My sister-in-law tried to get her six-month-old baby a job as a photo model, because she wanted nice pictures of the baby for free. But they said my niece was too old and fat. That's so wrong! They said they'd be willing to consider the baby if she would "drop two."

—*Cathryn Michon*

A new psychological disorder has been identified, called muscle dysmorphia. This is when bodybuilders think of themselves as scrawny and undeveloped. You can always tell who these guys are. They're the ones at the beach kicking sand in their own face.

—*Bill Maher*

Americans are getting stronger. Twenty years ago it took two people to carry ten dollars' worth of groceries. Today, a five-year-old can do it.

—*Henny Youngman*

You're never too fat or too thin; it's all in the people you're hanging with. If you're big, stick with people bigger than you, and they'll call you Slim. If you're skinny, go with people who are scrawny, and feel bulked up. See, I've just saved you from wasting thousands of hours and dollars on the gym.

—*Sinbad*

Piercing

When considering whether or not to have a metal stud put through your tongue, or your belly button, or your genitalia, take lightning into account.

—*Dennis Miller*

I met this Vietnamese kid who had his nose, tongue, and lip pierced, which he called body art. So I told him, "Hey, when your ancestors had metal all over their face, they called it shrapnel."

—*Wally Wang*

I'm in favor of self-mutilation and personal disfigurement. I've always said there's nothing like puncturing and perforating your skin in a dozen or so places in order to demonstrate your high self-esteem. When I see a young man decorating his scalp with a soldering iron, I think, "Now, there's a happy guy."

—*George Carlin*

Everyone's getting pierced these days. Maybe they'll get their parents pierced, too. I guess the winner will be the family who takes the longest to get through the metal detector.

—*Norman K.*

Pilot

I dated a pilot, he was a kamikaze. He was really bad at it, though. He kept landing.

—*Wendy Liebman*

I used to be an airline pilot. I got fired because I kept locking the keys in the plane. They caught me on an eighty-foot stepladder with a coat hanger.

—*Steven Wright*

Plants

I have no plants in my house. They won't live for me. Some of them don't even wait to die, they commit suicide. I once came home and found one hanging from a macramé noose, the pot kicked out from underneath. The note said, "I hate you, and your albums."

—*Jerry Seinfeld*

All the plants in my house are dead; I shot them last night. I was teasing them by watering them with ice cubes.

—*Steven Wright*

Plastic Surgery

I have a friend who got those new saline implants. She laid in the sun so long they evaporated. All she's got now is two double-D salt shakers. We make margaritas, people rub their glasses on her breasts.

—*Aisha Tyler*

I've never had plastic surgery. I still have my own real breasts. I know, because when I lay on my back they roll underneath my arms, and I look like a hammerhead shark.

—*Le Maire*

Police

When it rains really hard, I like to run stop signs, just to make cops get out of their cars. Why make the money if you can't enjoy spending it? Make him stand there in a big puddle. "You know why I stopped you?" "You know why I ran the sign?"

—*Drew Carey*

One time a cop pulled me over for running a stop sign. He said, "Didn't you see the stop sign?" I said, "Yeah, but I don't believe everything I read."

—*Steven Wright*

Up in Oregon a female police officer was fired because they found out she was selling Mary Kay cosmetics out of her squad car. They got suspicious when she described a suspect as tall, Caucasian, and an Autumn.

—*Bill Maher*

West Coast cops are obsessed with traffic. New York cops don't give a shit. You can be driving along the streets of Manhattan sixty miles an hour with a beer between your legs, seat belt flapping out the door, a big joint in your mouth, go through five red lights, pass a New York cop, and he'll yell, "Yo! Bring me a cup of coffee on your way back, okay?"

—*Richard Belzer*

In New York City, there was a big controversy because the police shot an unarmed black man. And now, they've announced a drive to attract more minorities to the police force. Good advertisement, huh? And I don't think the slogan is gonna help either, "If we can't beat you, join us."

—*Bill Maher*

Polite

You can say, "Can I use your bathroom?" and nobody really cares. But if you say, "I have to use the plop-plop machine," it always breaks the conversation.

—*Dave Attell*

I'm always putting my foot in my mouth. I met this woman recently, and I could have sworn she was pregnant. I think the rule is, don't guess at that ever, ever, ever.

—*Brian Regan*

I hate being polite to boring people. I'd much rather tell them, "Shut up! I have a great story I'm listening to in my own head, thank you very much. And please stop using up all the fresh air."

—*Gloria Brinkworth*

Politics

Move election day to April 15. Pay your taxes and hold elections on the same day. See if any of these duplicitous sons of bitches would try to get away with their crap, if we paid their salaries on the same day we voted for them.

—*Dennis Miller*

Congress has initiated legislation for a salary increase. The vote is expected to be split along party lines, with Republican members of Congress in favor of the measure, and Democratic members of Congress in favor of the measure.

—*Craig Kilborn*

Politicians are interested in people. Not that this is always a virtue. Fleas are interested in dogs.

—*P. J. O'Rourke*

Politics is so corrupt, even the dishonest people get screwed.

—*George Carlin*

Pat Buchanan says he's leaving the Republican Party for the Reform Party, whose current big star is Jesse Ventura. I don't know if Pat has the charisma to compete with Jesse, but he did do a little wrestling back in the early part of his career under the name Hulk Hitler.

—*Bill Maher*

George W. Bush claims to be a compassionate conservative. That's somebody who wants to feed the homeless by leaving the lid of the Dumpster open.

—*Jay Leno*

These conservatives are all in favor of the unborn, they'll do anything for the unborn. But once you're born, you're on your own. They're not interested in you until you reach military age. Conservatives want live babies, so they can raise them to be dead soldiers.

—*George Carlin*

Joke Stew

Dan Quayle warned Republicans that drifting away from conservative values is a recipe for defeat. By the way, the ingredients for this defeat recipe are two tablespoons of homophobia, a half cup of racial insensitivity, and just a hint of anti-abortion fervor.

—*Craig Kilborn*

Bill Clinton treated the truth like your mom treats the good china. There's never an occasion special enough to actually use it, although you take it out and look at it once in a while.

—*Dennis Miller*

Al Gore basically said that he created the Internet. Trent Lott, the majority leader, mocked him in the Senate by saying he invented the paper clip. And then Strom Thurmond pulled out the patent for fire.

—*Bill Maher*

There's nothing wrong with our foreign policy that faith, hope, and clarity couldn't cure.

—*Henny Youngman*

The Republicans, whose health care plan consists of Just Say No to Sickness.

—*Kevin Pollack*

The National Governors' Association welcomed Minnesota's governor Jesse Ventura, who arrived late, wearing a tasseled leather jacket and white boots. Yeah, that's how you want your governor dressing, like Tanya Tucker with a dash of gay stripper.

—*Colin Quinn*

There's actually a Nixon Center for Peace and Freedom in Washington. What's next? The Mike Tyson Center for Feminist Studies?

—*Norman K.*

I'm forty-nine and I don't have any political affiliation, but I'm thinking of becoming a Republican. If you're a Democrat and forty-nine, you're over the hill. But if you're a Republican, you're the youngest guy out there.

—*Jay Leno*

The Republicans keep talking about returning power to the states. Oh great, let's have more things run by the people who brought you the Department of Motor Vehicles.

—*Andy Kindler*

I think if we put enough money into medical research, we can find a cure for Republicanism sometime in the next millennium.

—*Jerry Rubin*

The Senate was holding hearings on deceptive sweepstakes practices. These companies target the elderly, making them think they're going to get a bunch of money, when in reality they never see any of it. The most popular of these scams is called Social Security.

—*Colin Quinn*

I must have been asleep when they elected Al Sharpton as the black representative. He must be the only leader in history to show up to a rally wearing a tight red velour sweat suit with a roller in the front of his hair. And what's up with the brother's hair? It looks like he swallowed James Brown.

—*Damon Wayans*

Strom Thurmond was admitted to the hospital for the third time in a month. It's sad to see someone you respect and admire pass on, and even sadder to see someone you loath hang on by a thread for several decades. Strom served in the U.S. Senate for thirty-four years, or as he liked to say, one for every state in the union. Never swayed by thought or progress, a staunch defender of the classic values, like segregation, witch-hunting, and alchemy, Strom was always tireless, unbowed, and working for a better yesterday.

—*Bill Maher*

The hot new movie on video is the story of Kenneth Starr's future with the Republican Party, *The Waterboy.*

—Colin Quinn

On election day I stay home. Because if you vote, you have no right to complain. You elect dishonest, incompetent people, they get in office and screw everything up—you caused the problem. I am in no way responsible, and have every right to complain as loud as I want to about the mess you people created.

—George Carlin

It doesn't surprise me that Washington, D.C., is such a sexist place; it's a town that lives in the shadow of the Washington Monument, the world's largest dick. And there's never going to be a woman president, until somebody digs a seven-hundred-foot tunnel honoring Eleanor Roosevelt.

—Cathryn Michon

I'm offended by political jokes. Too often they get elected.

—Henny Youngman

If God had wanted us to vote, he would have given us candidates.

—*Jay Leno*

Too bad the only people who know how to run the country are busy driving cabs and cutting hair.

—*George Burns*

Pornography

Men love to watch two women make love. I wonder, does this turn them on, or are they just trying to figure out how to do it right?

—*Joy Behar*

I don't like porn, because I'm self-centered and don't get anything that doesn't involve me directly. I can't even watch the food channel, because I'm like, "Where's my baked Alaska?" If I were watching a porn movie I'd probably be like, "Where's my really ugly guy from New Jersey with a hairy back, and a bizarrely large penis?"

—*Cathryn Michon*

There's a new porno movie, *John Wayne Bobbitt, Uncut.* Y'know, if that's what it takes to get into the porno business, I withdraw my application.

—*Norman K.*

Power Outage

One time the power went out in my house, and I had to use the flash on my camera to see my way around. I made a sandwich, and took fifty pictures of my face. The neighbors thought there was lightning in my house.

—*Steven Wright*

Prayer

Why is it when we talk to God we're said to be praying, but when God talks to us we're schizophrenic?

—*Lily Tomlin*

When I was a kid, I used to pray every night for a new bicycle. Then I realized that the Lord, in his wisdom, didn't work that way. So I stole one, and asked him to forgive me.

—*Emo Philips*

I squirm when I see athletes praying before a game. Don't they realize that if God took sports seriously he never would have created George Steinbrenner?

—*Mark Russell*

Pregnancy

The sonogram. We had fun looking for early traces of family resemblance. "Gee, honey, it looks just like your mother, if she were bald, had no eyelids, and was floating in amniotic fluid." "Yeah, but from this side, it looks like your father. Presuming, of course, he was a Hawaiian prawn."

—*Paul Reiser*

Natural childbirth class. A great place to find chicks, if you're into the full-figured gals. And you can be reasonably sure these girls put out.

—*Jonathan Katz*

Procrastination

My mother said, "You won't amount to anything because you procrastinate." I said, "Just wait."

—*Judy Tenuta*

My friend Winnie is a procrastinator. He didn't get his birthmark until he was eight years old.

—*Steven Wright*

Psychic

Psychics should be licensed. We could give them the regular DMV test, only with silver dollars and pizza dough over the eyes. If you can parallel park like that, you're a psychic.

—*Jerry Seinfeld*

TV is dangerous, especially after midnight. I think, "Let's see if these psychics really work." Wake one up at four A.M. But if she's not asleep, you got to wonder: "If you're so psychic, why can't you see your way to a better life than sitting by the phone all night long?"

—*Sinbad*

Punishment

Alabama has become the first state to revive chain gangs. And they vow not to stop there. They intend to review the lyrics of every single Sam Cooke song, for additional improvements to the criminal justice system.

—*Johnny Robish*

Prisons are big business. We put more people in jail than Iran or Iraq. Twenty years ago, we spent twice as much on colleges as prisons. Now we spend more on prisons. We now consider jail our low-income housing program.

—*Norman K.*

When my dad went to prison, I lost my faith in God. It's ironic, because my dad found the Lord in prison. God was serving ten to twenty-five for creating Jesse Helms.

—*Lesley Wake*

Racism

People always want to judge you based on your ethnic background. It's stupid. For instance, if a white guy likes rap, he's trying to be black. If a black guy gets a job, he's trying to be white.

—*Aisha Tyler*

I was with a Japanese friend in New York, and a group of teenagers ran up to us screaming, "Fucking Chinos ruin everything!" We weren't upset at first, because we weren't sure if they were talking about us, or the pants. Because they could be either really racist, or really fashion conscious.

—*Margaret Cho*

Why is it always the ugliest white people with this message: "The white race is superior"? Jesus, holy cow, you've got gills and a pointed head! You should date around. Date outside your immediate family, is my advice to you. Seek out the swarthy-skinned, almond-eyed people, I think you'll find them a refreshing dip in the gene pool.

—*Greg Proops*

Everything exploits the Indians. *F Troop,* the Mazola commercial, the Cleveland Indians. Remember the Indian chief with the tear in his eye, supposedly crying for the environment? He wasn't crying for the environment, he was crying because somebody took his land, then raped and killed his wife. The ozone was the least of his worries.

—*Chris Rock*

White racists don't make any sense. Many of them are deeply religious, but believe that when they die, they'll go to a place where there are only other white people. Which means that heaven for these crackers will be Denny's, Texaco, or Motel 6.

—*Wally Wang*

Just what is reverse racism? Is there something white people are not getting? Reverse racism is like Mike Tyson saying, "It's not fair; me always having to fight the heavy guys. From now on, I only want to fight lightweights."

—*Chris Rock*

Refrigerator

I cleaned my refrigerator out the other day, hadn't done that for a while. Found a milk carton with the Lindbergh baby on it.

—*John Mendoza*

Relationships

Irrational crushes, infatuations, or obsessions. Whatever you want to label it, it's important to reach out to others.

—*Janeane Garofalo*

We've been talking about getting a third person in our relationship, you know, a three-way. Could be a woman, could be a man; it's not for sex—we just need a witness. I'm looking for someone with good hearing, good eyesight, and an excellent memory, who would tell her what really happened.

—*Marga Gomez*

My boyfriend had no trouble committing . . . adultery.

—*Wendy Liebman*

I wish our lovers treated us like apartments. They'd have to give us thirty days' notice before they left us, and they'd have to leave us in the same condition they found us in.

—*Denise Munro Robb*

You always know when the relationship is over. Little things start grating on your nerves, "Would you please stop that! That breathing in and out, it's so repetitious!"

—*Ellen DeGeneres*

Relationships are hard. It's like a full-time job, and we should treat it like one. If your boyfriend or girlfriend wants to leave you, they should give you two weeks' notice. There should be severance pay, and before they leave you, they have to find you a temp.

—*Bob Ettinger*

Religion

I go to an atheist church. They have crippled guys who stand up and say they were once crippled—and they still are.

—*Paula Poundstone*

The Amish are now having the same kind of problems everywhere else does. Four teenagers were arrested for violence. They broke windows, they overturned buggies. They could tell it was these boys because the graffiti on the silo said, "Ye suck."

—Bill Maher

I spent a week at a Buddhist monastic retreat, where I sat silently for hours at a time in an uncomfortable position trying to shatter my ego. Why bother? Two minutes with my wife and kids does the same thing.

—Brian Koffman

Catholicism. What can you say about a religion that makes a sin out of sex, and a sacred act out of drinking alcohol?

—Atom

I was raised Roman Catholic, and according to the Catholic Church it's okay to be homosexual, as long as you don't practice homosexuality. Which is interesting, because I think it's okay to be Catholic as long as you don't practice Catholicism.

—Bob Smith

I grew up a Catholic, which is good. It gives you something to work out the rest of your life.

—*Steven Sweeney*

They're modernizing some things in the Church. When they serve the wafer in communion, they also have a salad bar.

—*Bill Maher*

I've always wondered why they don't put a dab of frosting on communion wafers. Some powdered sugar? I mean, could anyone think God would be opposed to some flavoring? Does anyone think he's up there eating those wafers?

—*Louie Anderson*

In Catholic grade school in religion class, I was told to scoot over in my desk and make room for my guardian angel to sit down. Because, apparently, my guardian angel was a lazy fat ass with the inability to hover.

—*Kathleen Madigan*

I got suspended from Catholic school. At an eighth-grade dance I was told I was dancing too close to a girl. Father said, "Leave a little room for the Holy Ghost!" And I said, "Are you kidding? After what he did to Mary?"

—*Atom*

I'd rather meet an ax murderer than a born-again Christian. At least an ax murderer will eventually leave you alone.

—*Barry Steiger*

I've been having a hard time with my Christianity lately, because of all the nepotism. After a hard day of being rejected in show business, the last thing I want to do is come home and worship a savior who got the job because his dad owns the whole freakin' universe. To me, Jesus is just the Tori Spelling of saviors.

—*Cathryn Michon*

An interesting item in the paper. It said, people who go to church live longer than those who don't go to church regularly. Pat Robertson jumped on this. He's putting out a bumper sticker that says, "Jesus saves, and reduces cholesterol."

—*Bill Maher*

Say what you will about the Ten Commandments, you must always come back to the pleasant fact that there are only ten of them.

—*H. L. Mencken*

Thou shall not kill. Thou shall not commit adultery. Don't eat pork. I'm sorry, what was the last one? Don't eat pork? Is that the word of God, or is that pigs trying to outsmart everybody?

—*Jon Stewart*

Most unselfish religion: the Jehovah's Witnesses. They think only 144,000 people are going to heaven. If you believed that, would you go door to door trying to get new converts? I'd be keeping that a big secret. "I hear there are only eight seats left, shut up!"

—*Kathleen Madigan*

Do you know what you get when you cross a Jehovah's Witness with an atheist? Someone who knocks on your door for no apparent reason.

—*Guy Owen*

The reason I like the Jehovah's Witnesses is that they pay their dues. They stand out in the wind and the rain, and they hand the first passerby the *Watchtower*. And they watch as he drops it in the nearest wastepaper basket. Then they go to the wastebasket, shake the pamphlet out, and wait for the next passerby. They've been in existence since 1812, and they've only had to use six pamphlets.

—*David Steinberg*

Jesus had twelve disciples who followed him wherever he went. How annoying is that? Do you think he ever turned to them and said, "What?"

—*Jon Stewart*

A Mississippi school board is being sued by a fifteen-year-old student. They said he couldn't wear the Star of David to school, because it's a gang symbol. They don't know a lot about Jews in Mississippi. Except they think they're one of the toughest gangs, because to get initiated you have to cut your penis.

—*Bill Maher*

If there is a Lord, he truly does work in mysterious ways. A few nights ago at work, I returned to one of my tables after the customers had just left, and all that remained were some crumbs, some scattered cups, and a leaflet that read, "Jesus Saves." Maybe so, but he sure as hell doesn't tip.

—*Brock Cohen*

Mormons are very organized. I had this neighbor Mrs. Mabey who stocked canned goods in her basement, so she could be prepared for when Christ returns to Earth. Because apparently what Christ is looking for is creamed corn.

—*Natasha Ahanin*

Oral Roberts. I have respect for any religious leader who can make it to the top with so obscene a first name. I'd always thought Oral was a nickname you might get for being really good at something.

—*David Steinberg*

If you flip the pages of the Old Testament in one direction you get Jesus riding a horse, and in the other direction, a fat lady with a Hula Hoop. Back then everyone thought she would be the famous one.

—*Gilbert Gottfried*

I do not believe in an afterlife. Although I am bringing a change of underwear.

—*Woody Allen*

Some people believe in reincarnation. If I come back, I want to be a famous racehorse, they have it made. Free room and board, plenty of exercise. The best part is the retirement plan. "Looks like it's time to put him out to stud." I have a similar retirement plan at my job, except here they screw me.

—*Joel Warshaw*

Go look for consistency in religion. Catholics and Christians are against abortions and against homosexuals.

But who has less abortions than homosexuals? Here is an entire class of people guaranteed not to have an abortion. Leave these people alone, for Christ's sake.

—*George Carlin*

Organized religion has taken a turn for the worst. Just the other day I drove by "The Church of the Seven or So Commandments: Pastor Bill Clinton and the Reverend O. J. Simpson."

—*Sue Bova*

Mormons can have multiple wives. The funny thing is, most guys I know don't even want one.

—*Joel Warshaw*

Remarriage

Hard to replace a great man. Coretta never met another man, because how you gonna add up to Martin Luther King? Martin was the greatest civil rights leader ever, and your ass is working second shift at the post office. You know she'd never let you forget it, "My first man had a dream, and you don't even have a plan. He had a holiday, that you go to work on."

—*D. L. Hughley*

Restaurants

When I go to a restaurant I always ask the manager, "Give me a table near a waiter."

—*Henny Youngman*

I went to this restaurant last night that was set up like a big buffet in the shape of a Ouija board. You'd think about what kind of food you want, and the table would move across the floor to it.

—*Steven Wright*

Eating out is very expensive. I was in one restaurant, they didn't even have prices on the menu. Just pictures of faces with different expressions of horror.

—*Rita Rudner*

There's a pizza place near where I live that sells only slices. In the back you can see a guy tossing a triangle in the air.

—*Steven Wright*

Why does Sea World have a seafood restaurant? I'm halfway through my fishburger and I realize, "Oh my God, I could be eating a slow learner."

—*Lynda Montgomery*

You go to a nice restaurant, they put the check in a little book. What is this, the story of a bill? "Once upon a time, somebody ordered a salad." There's a little gold tassel hanging down. Am I graduating from the restaurant? Should I put this on the rearview mirror of my Camaro?

—*Jerry Seinfeld*

Reunions

I run into this guy I went to high school with I haven't seen in ten years, and I ask him what's going on. And he says, "I finally got an amp for my bass!" Which answers a lot of other questions, like, "Are you still smoking a lot of pot? Living in your mom's basement?"

—*Dave Attell*

I went to the thirtieth reunion of my preschool. I didn't want to go, because I've put on like a hundred pounds.

—*Wendy Liebman*

Roommate

Roommates are tough. Even if you shared an apartment with the Pope, I guarantee that three weeks into it you'd be going, "Hey, you mind picking up the cape, man? And quit leaving the papal miter on the kitchen counter."

—*Jeff Foxworthy*

I had a roommate with Tourette's syndrome, the disease where you shout out profanity at random. I loved this guy. I'd have him answer the door whenever a Jehovah's Witness knocked.

—Wally Wang

Three roommates, and nobody washes dishes in my apartment. I looked in the cupboard the other day, it was empty. I had to get out my Yahtzee game for a clean cup. Next time I'm thirsty I'll be drinking out of the thimble from the Monopoly game.

—Dobie Maxwell

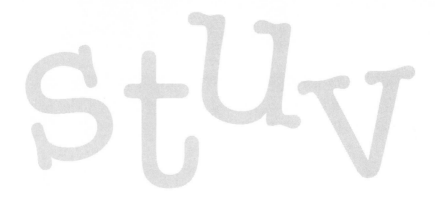

Safety

It's the kids today I'm worried about, their lives are going to be so soft. I don't recall any overt safety features on anything when I was a kid. Electrical outlets didn't have covers. That was pretty much trial by error. "Hey, don't stick your finger in that . . . oh Jesus. Look at your steaming, curly little head."

—*Elvira Kurt*

The National Highway Safety Administration has developed a whole family of crash test dummies, which seems kind of irresponsible. What kind of family life are those child-sized dummies gonna have? Every day your parents are involved in two or three major car wrecks. Every time the phone rings, "Pop? You hit the wall again? You didn't have a seat belt on? How's Mom?"

—*Jay Leno*

Safety was not a big thing when I was growing up. A seat belt was something that got in the way: "Ma, the seat belt is digging into my back." "Stuff it down into the seat. And roll those windows up, you're letting the smoke out."

—*Margaret Smith*

School

My kindergarten teacher hated me. She used to find any excuse to pick on me, especially during nap time. Like I'm the only guy who sleeps naked.

—*Brian Kiley*

My first-grade teacher said, "Okay, Mark, tell us everything you know about the letter H." I said, "That's Jesus' middle name."

—*Mark Lundholm*

In elementary school, in case of fire you have to line up quietly in a single-file line from smallest to tallest. What is the logic? Do tall people burn slower?

—*Warren Hutcherson*

229

In elementary school during Student Government Week, I was Coroner for the Day.

—*Richard Lewis*

I liked school. The best part was to get those new school supplies. The challenge was to convince the smaller kids that I was going to give them back.

—*Jim Rez*

It's a myth that you will be able to help your children with their homework. I'm taking remedial math so I can help my son make it to the third grade.

—*Sinbad*

My wife won't send my youngest girl to Catholic school, because the teachers hit the kids. So we sent her to public school, where the kids hit the teachers.

—*Colin Quinn*

My school colors were clear. We used to say, "I'm not naked, I'm in the band."

—*Steven Wright*

I had a typical high school romance. I was a cheerleader, and he was on the faculty.

—*Wendy Liebman*

Back in high school, my buddies tried to put the make on anything that moved. I told them, "Why limit yourselves?"

—*Emo Philips*

In high school I had the worst case of acne ever. Although it really helped my grades because I never had those pesky boys dragging me away from the books. And I got extra credit in geology, because my teacher thought I had a model of the Grand Canyon on my face.

—*Ann Oelschlager*

I studied the Constitution in high school, learned the Fourth Amendment. That's the one concerned with search and seizure. For example, if my mother had searched my room, she would've had a seizure.

—*Norman K.*

A lot of stuff in school you don't appreciate till you get to be older. Little things, like being spanked every day by a middle-aged woman. Stuff you'd pay good money for later in life.

—*Emo Philips*

Science

Genetic scientists say that one day it will be possible to grow new body parts, like new breasts and new hands. It's going to be a huge moneymaker, because you know that as soon as women grow another breast, men will want another hand.

—*Jay Leno*

Researchers at Johns Hopkins announced an incredible breakthrough in shoe science. Solving a puzzle that has eluded scientists for decades, they reported that it's the left sandal that's the flip, and the right sandal that's the flop.

—*Craig Kilborn*

Scientists say that your nose and ears continue to grow over the course of your lifetime. If that's the case, Evander Holyfield might want to fight Tyson again just to get a trim.

—*Jay Leno*

Self-Esteem

I know a guy who has such low self-esteem that he keeps his keys on him when he walks through the airport metal detector, just to get some acknowledgment.

—*Daniel Lybra*

Sex

When my daughter was six she started asking embarrassing questions. Luckily, we had gotten her two hamsters, and about a week later she had four hamsters. So I explained that when a boy hamster and a girl hamster love each other, and make a commitment, they can have baby hamsters. A week after that she had twenty hamsters, so I had to tell her about incest.

—*Jonathan Katz*

What's the sexiest four-word sentence in the English language? It's when a southern woman says, "Hey, y'all, I'm drunk."

—*Jeff Foxworthy*

After making love I said to my girl, "Was it good for you, too?" And she said, "I don't think that was good for anybody."

—*Garry Shandling*

Women need a reason to have sex. Men just need a place.

—*Billy Crystal*

Making love to a woman is like buying real estate: location, location, location.

—*Carol Leifer*

I told my girlfriend that Dr. Ruth compared men to a sexual microwave: they start fast and finish fast. And women are more like Crock-Pots: they take a long time to heat up, but can cook for hours. My girlfriend said, "Yeah, and you're like an old toaster that heats for ten seconds before it pops up."

—*Joe Ditzel*

There's a double standard, even today. A man can sleep around and sleep around, and nobody asks any questions. A woman, you make nineteen or twenty mistakes, right away you're a tramp.

—*Joan Rivers*

Sex in your twenties, "Yes, yes, yes—again." Sex in your thirties, "Ow, my hip."

—*Caroline Rhea*

My mother and I had different attitudes toward sex. She said, "Whatever you do, never sleep with a man until he buys you a house." It worked for her. And I got a swing set out of the deal.

—*Judy Brown*

The only way to really have safe sex is to abstain. From drinking.

—*Wendy Liebman*

It seems like we hear more talk about the threesome in sex. And when I was single that was sincerely never a fantasy of mine. It was never like, "How could I wake up with *two* disappointed ladies tomorrow?"

—*Bobcat Goldthwait*

My mother is sixty, and her whole life she only slept with one guy. She won't tell me who.

—*Wendy Liebman*

Into bondage? I am. What I do when I'm in the mood is tie her up, and gag her, and go into the living room and watch football.

—*Tom Arnold*

I tried group sex. Now I have a new problem. I don't know who to thank.

—*Rodney Dangerfield*

I wonder, is pain always sexual for S and M people? If they're walking down the street, and they stub their toe, do they go, "Ow! I'm so horny."

—*Suzanne Westenhoefer*

I tried phone sex once, I did. I'll be honest with you. I got my penis stuck in the nine.

—*Kevin Meaney*

Phone sex, my worst fantasy. "You're thinking dirty thoughts?" "Yeah." "Okay, your mother wants to talk to you."

—*Robert Schimmel*

During sex my wife always wants to talk to me. Just the other night she called me from a hotel.

—*Rodney Dangerfield*

I once made love for an hour and five minutes. It was on the day they push the clock ahead.

—*Garry Shandling*

I was having a lot of sexual problems. So a couple Amish friends came over for an erection raising.

—*Richard Lewis*

My husband says, "Roseanne, don't you think we ought to talk about our sexual problems?" Like I'm gonna turn off *Wheel of Fortune* for that.

—Roseanne

I tell ya, I got no sex life. My dog watched me in the bedroom, to learn how to beg. He also taught my wife how to roll over and play dead.

—Rodney Dangerfield

In a survey for *Modern Maturity* magazine, men over seventy-five said they had sex once a week. Which proves that old guys lie about sex, too.

—Irv Gilman

Shopping

I'm a shopaholic. I especially like to shop for shoes, because I don't have to take off the rest of my clothes. But if I do, I get a much bigger discount.

—Bea Carroll

Here's how a guy shops. He's standing outside. He goes, "I'm cold." He goes in the store, buys the coat, walks out. "I'm not cold anymore. Shopping is over."

—Ritch Shydner

She's a bargain hunter, my mom. The other day she left with a few Coke containers, and came back with a sit-down mower.

—*Margaret Smith*

I went shopping for feminine protection. I decided on a thirty-eight revolver.

—*Karen Ripley*

I bought this hemp lotion from the Body Shop. It smelled great, so I rubbed it all over my body. An hour later, my thighs wanted a brownie.

—*Lesley Wake*

Layaway I've hated since I was small. Go to the store, pick out the cool pair of pants, and Mama messed you up. "We'll put in a dollar a week." A dollar a week! It can take a whole life to pay off. You visit your clothes and watch them go out of style. Then, fifty-five years old, "I'm picking up the burgundy sharkskin pants, boys' size six."

—*Sinbad*

The problem with the mall garage is that everything looks the same. What they need to do is name the levels like, "Your mother's a whore." You would remember that. "I know where we're parked. We're in 'Your mother's a whore.' And your friend would go, "No we're not. We're in 'My father's an abusive alcoholic.' "

—*Jerry Seinfeld*

Shower

A lot of couples shower together. It's supposed to be romantic and sensual. Truth? One of you is not getting water. One of you, therefore, is not taking a shower. One of you is having a great time, one of you is going, "You got a sweater up there? Something with a hood would be nice. I would get it, but my ass is frozen to the wall here."

—*Paul Reiser*

I tell ya, cleanliness, that's what's important. But some people are too clean. Like my uncle Louie. He used to take five showers a day, four baths a day. And when he died, as a tribute to my uncle's cleanliness, the entire funeral procession went through a car wash.

—*Rodney Dangerfield*

Someone gave me one of those gift sets, has the cologne, aftershave, soap-on-a-rope. I guess I need soap-on-a-rope for those times I'm in the shower, and want to hang myself.

—*Jerry Seinfeld*

Single

The thing I hate about living alone is living alone. I have way too many frivolous conversations with the 411 operator.

—*Sue Bova*

It's pretty lonely and sad to be single. Every night was the same for me, I'd go home and curl up in bed with my favorite book. Well, actually it was a magazine.

—*Tom Arnold*

I've been single so long, I open the refrigerator door, and Mrs. Butterworth is starting to look good to me.

—*Dobie Maxwell*

Being single is tough, especially if you're trying to meet someone in a bar. I think people in bars should be required to wear collars, like dogs. That way you'd get their basic information right up front. Name, where they live, and if they've gotten their shots.

—*Joel Warshaw*

Sleep

When I woke up this morning my girlfriend asked me, "Did you sleep good?" I said, "No, I made a few mistakes."

—*Steven Wright*

I love to sleep. It's the best of both worlds. You get to be alive, and unconscious.

—*Rita Rudner*

I decided to take better control of my life, and make sure that less things go wrong, so I've been sleeping for twenty hours a day. I figured that in four hours even I couldn't screw up that many things. And if I have to parallel park, that leaves me with just the one hour to kill.

—*Paula Poundstone*

I don't care how big the bed is, or how soft or hard it is. It's impossible to sleep in a hotel. Just try to close those curtains. That must be a big joke with the contractors. All of them leave that one-inch slit down the middle. No matter where you lie, the light finds you. Like that picture of Jesus where the eyes follow you.

—*Louie Anderson*

Smoking

Smoking is, as far as I'm concerned, the entire point of being an adult.

—*Fran Lebowitz*

The uses of tobacco aren't obvious right off the bat. You shred it up, put it on a piece of paper, roll it up, and stick it between your lips . . . and set fire to it. Then you inhale the smoke. You could stand in front of your fireplace and have the same thing going.

—*Bob Newhart*

I don't smoke. I don't even understand what the point is. All I can tell is that these people are addicted to blowing smoke out of their faces. It's not even a good trick. If you could blow smoke out of your face without everyone knowing where it came from, that would be impressive.

—*Brad Stine*

This guy is puffing on a cigar the size of God's ego, and he's blowing the smoke in my face. I said, "Excuse me, but if I wanted to shorten my life, I'd date you."

—*Judy Tenuta*

I don't let men smoke in my apartment. But if I have a woman over she can barbecue a goat.

—*Todd Barry*

I stopped smoking cigarettes, because people were always coming up to me saying, "Miss, your smoke is bothering me." "So what, it's *killing* me."

—*Wendy Liebman*

If you're saying you didn't know cigarettes were bad for you, you're lying through that hole in your trachea.

—*Dennis Miller*

Nicotine Anonymous is for people who want to stop smoking. When you get a craving for a cigarette, you call another member. He comes over, and you get drunk together.

—*Henny Youngman*

You nonsmokers are the pissiest people. You're so demanding about your opportunity for clean air space. How can I possibly respect you? You don't have the nerve to take your own life in a horrible way, slowly and painfully, over a great number of years.

—*Stephanie Hodge*

I finally quit smoking by using the patch. I put six of them over my mouth.

—*Wendy Liebman*

Smoking cures weight problems. Eventually.

—*Steven Wright*

Tobacco giant Philip Morris is recalling its top-selling brands of cigarettes because of a defect. They made a batch that didn't cause cancer.

—*Johnny Robish*

Sorority

Being in a sorority was like flying coach. Both had bitchy women telling me all I was allowed to eat was a small bag of pretzels and a diet Coke.

—*Stephanie Schiern*

Spanking

I remember the days when it was fashionable to spank your child. My father would say to me, "This hurts me worse than it does you." I wanted to say, "Then you bend over, and I'll lighten your emotional load, buddy."

—*Liz Sells*

Never raise your hands to your kids. It leaves your groin unprotected.

—*Red Buttons*

Sports

Taking up a new sport, I have always subscribed to the rule, Whatever you lack in skill, make up for in silly accessories. "How's your tennis game?" "Not great. But I have a hat with a tiny solar-powered fan that keeps me cool, and a racket the size of an outdoor grill."

—*Paul Reiser*

If it weren't for baseball, many kids wouldn't know what a millionaire looks like.

—*Phyllis Diller*

I've been playing a lot of basketball lately, down at the playground. It's tough to get into games down there, that's how good those guys are. Some days, the only way I get on the court is when they get called in for nap time.

—*Brock Cohen*

Today I watched bowling. Not because I like bowling, but for the cheerleaders.

—*Howie Mandel*

I've always liked the two months before Mike Tyson fights when we got to listen to every idiot like my 5'9" brother say, "I'd fight him for a million dollars." I bet you would. And then twenty years from now we'd get your follow-up interview on CNN, "I'm eating solid foods again. And I can squeeze the ball!"

—*Kathleen Madigan*

George Foreman is forty-nine years old. What's he doing boxing? You know when you sock him in the gut, he pees a little.

—*Margaret Smith*

To fight inequality, female athletes have to start committing more crimes. Jennifer Capriati got caught with some pot. That's nothing. Get with the program: assault, murder, ear biting, date rape. Put all the women athletes together, and they have a shorter rap sheet than the Dallas Cowboys.

—*Norman K.*

If a man watches three football games in a row, he should be declared legally dead.

—*Erma Bombeck*

It's reassuring to see that colleges are putting the emphasis on education again. One school has gotten so strict they won't give a football player his letter, unless he can tell which one it is.

—*Henny Youngman*

The hardest part of being a professional football player is, on the one hand you're a millionaire, on the other, they blow a whistle and you have to run around after a football. To me, the whole idea of being a millionaire is: somebody throws a football at me—maybe I catch it, maybe I don't. I'd think you could get someone to hand you the ball, at that point.

—*Jerry Seinfeld*

Anyone can be a golf announcer. All you have to do is use that voice you use when you call in sick at work. "I won't be coming in today, I have a golf game to announce."

—*Mike Rowe*

Everyone plays golf now, which is a lot like going to a strip club. You get all charged up, pay big money to hang out on a beautiful course, and start drinking early. Eighteen holes later, you're plastered and frustrated, and most of your balls are missing.

—*Tim Allen*

I watched the Indy 500. And I was thinking—if they left earlier they wouldn't have to go so fast.

—*Steven Wright*

Karate is a form of martial arts in which people who have had years and years of training can, using only their hands and feet, make some of the worst movies in the history of the world.

—*Dave Barry*

Scuba diving. A great activity where your main goal is, Just Don't Die. So Mr. Scuba Guy takes me to the store to buy everything I need. I got the waterproof watch and the waterproof wallet. In case I meet a sea turtle who can break a fifty.

—*Jerry Seinfeld*

Cross-country skiing is great if you live in a small country.

—*Steven Wright*

I went snowboarding today. Well, actually, I went careening off a mountain on a giant tongue depressor.

—*Paul Provenza*

You know those sports fantasy camps where you can play baseball for a week with former major leaguers? There's this new sports fantasy package updated for the nineties. You get to smoke crack with Lawrence Taylor, pick up hookers with Darryl Strawberry, and spend a night in jail with Mike Tyson.

—*Jack Archey*

Brothers are now conquering sports normally dominated by rich white people. We could take over polo, too, if they'd let a brother put a horse on layaway.

—*Chris Rock*

Stamps

The United States Postal Service and Mattel toys have teamed up to create a new Barbie postage stamp. Like the Elvis stamp, there will be two versions. The first being "Young Hot Cheerleader Barbie," followed by "Older, Overweight, I Never Thought My Life Would Be Like This, Bitter High School Reunion Barbie."

—*Craig Kilborn*

Star Wars

My friends JT and Eric are Star Wars maniacs, and live their lives through the Force. Which is not very useful in the ordinary, grown-up world. I don't need a guy to blow up the Death Star. I'll settle for any Jedi who can remember to come back from the grocery store with Tampax, instead of pork rinds.

—*Lesley Wake*

Stores

When I was a kid, I went to the store and asked the guy, "Do you have any toy train schedules?"

—*Steven Wright*

I don't imagine there are a lot of jobs easier than being a baby-store salesman, simply because you can't negotiate with them. If he says, "You don't *need* the high chair with the extrasafe support lock, but it is *safer*," what are you going to say? "Thank you, but we're gamblers by nature, and are curious to see if our infant will do as you predict, slide right out on his head, crashing violently onto the hardwood floor. That's something we'd like to see."

—*Paul Reiser*

My local Ralph's got a makeover. Now it has everything— florist, bakery, and everything is color coordinated. It looks like the Sharper Image grocery. But what bothers me most is their black shopping carts. They really bugged me, until I realized it was a Lexus for street people.

—*Eileen Courtney*

Strip Club

They opened up a strip bar in my neighborhood. Big sign out front, TOTALLY NUDE. I thought they meant to get in. So, I'm standing in line . . .

—*Margaret Smith*

Student Loan

I left college owing eighty thousand dollars in student loans. My mom tells me, "Just think of it as a mortgage." Yeah, and I can wallpaper my cardboard box with the interest statements.

—*Stephanie Schiern*

The student loan director from my bank called. He said, "You've missed seventeen payments, and the university never received the seventeen thousand dollars. We'd like to know what happened to the money." I said, "Mr. Jones, I'll give it to you straight. I gave the money to my friend Slick, and he built a nuclear weapon with it. And I'd appreciate it if you'd never call again."

—*Steven Wright*

Sunblock

We use a really strong sunblock when we go to the beach with the kids because we're always afraid of cancer. It's SPF 80: you squeeze the tube, and a sweater comes out.

—*Lew Schneider*

Superman

That last Superman series was really stupid. Every bad guy had kryptonite. It was a dime a dozen. "You wanna take out Superman? Yeah, I got something for ya. That'll be $3.50." Superman is frustrated. He's like, "Stop right there. Oh damn, you too? I quit."

—*Dominic Dierkes*

Talk

The opposite of talking isn't listening. The opposite of talking is waiting.

—*Fran Lebowitz*

We need a twelve-step group for compulsive talkers. They could call it On Anon Anon.

—*Paula Poundstone*

Women will gab at each other for fifty-seven hours, breaking down every emotional thing they're going through into nuances. A man will sit down with his buddy and his buddy will ask, "What's up with your wife?" The man will mumble, "Oh, man, she's tripping." End of analysis.

—*Sinbad*

Tarzan

Remember Tarzan? Big ol' hunk, swinging in the jungle, scaring the natives. Who were all black. Ain't it funny that this white guy, who was raised by a monkey, could control all those black folks? Daryl Gates could've used his ass during the L.A. riots.

—*Whoopi Goldberg*

Taste

You ever notice whenever you're with someone and they taste something that tastes bad, they always want you to taste it immediately. "This is disgusting. Taste it."

Ellen DeGeneres

Taxes

Worried about an audit? Always avoid what the IRS considers to be a red flag. For example, you have some money left in your bank account after paying taxes.

—*Jay Leno*

I screwed up my taxes last year. Instead of sending my return to the IRS, I sent it to the IRA. I had to pay a late penalty, and my apartment was firebombed.

—*Jack Archey*

The IRS sent back my tax return saying I owed eight hundred dollars. I said, "If you'll notice, I sent a paper clip with my return. Given what you've been paying for things lately, that should more than make up the difference."

—*Emo Philips*

Teacher

As a teacher, I tried to make my lesson plans relate to real life. It's important for kids to see connections. "Johnny, you got a sixty-five on this test. That's a D, and it's also the speed limit on the freeway! Uh oh, Suzie got the speed limit in a residential area."

—*Lesley Wake*

My wife is a teacher; it's really weird to live with a teacher. I'd be on the phone, doodling on a piece of paper, leave the house, come back in two hours, and that same piece of paper is now on the refrigerator with the words "Good work!" and a big smiley face on it.

—*Lew Schneider*

Technology

My parents were terrified of technology. No blender, no microwave, no power lawn mower, no television. They were like a suburban Jewish version of the Unabomber. And equally guilty, in their own way.

—*Norman K.*

Telephone

I plugged my phone in where the blender used to be. I called someone. They went, "Aaaaahhhh . . ."

—*Steven Wright*

Remember that as a teenager you are in the last stage of your life when you will be happy to hear the phone is for you.

—*Fran Lebowitz*

Therapy

I'm in therapy now. I used to be in denial. Which is a lot cheaper.

—*Robin Greenspan*

I hate marriage counselors. This is the biggest scam in the world. Someone figured out a way that women can do the things they love best at the same time, talk and spend money.

—*Damon Wayans*

If the marriage therapist irritates both of you, you can get some temporary zip back in your relationship if you team up and fight with her. That gives you some fresh sport for your money. After all, you can fight with each other for free on your own time.

—*Sinbad*

In my family, everyone is seeing a psychologist, except my mother. She creates the patients.

—*Stephanie Schiern*

I've been talking about my family with my therapist for so long that she now has her own problems with these people. Last week, I was talking about my mother and my therapist said, "Look, I don't want to hear another thing from that woman."

—*Sarah Citron*

Working as a psychologist is a lot like walking my dog. I coax, I pull, and then I finish by picking up the crap.

—*Gloria Brinkworth*

My aunt asked me, "You're a homosexual? Are you seeing a psychiatrist?" "No," I said, "I'm seeing a lieutenant in the army."

—*Bob Smith*

My mom has her own psychological problems. We just had to enroll her in Shoulder Pads Anonymous.

—*Stephanie Schiern*

Psychiatrist. A Jewish doctor who can't stand the sight of blood.

—*Henny Youngman*

Psychology is just psychiatry light, without all the drugs, additives, and preservatives. In psychology, you talk openly about your hopes, fears, and aspirations. In psychiatry, you're so pumped full of drugs, the thought of all that crap gives you the giggles.

—*Joel Warshaw*

Do you realize they have psychiatrists for dogs now? That in and of itself can screw up a dog.

—*Dennis Miller*

I started seeing a therapist. She didn't know I was seeing her. That was kinda fun.

—*Dana Snow*

Thinking

Men always scratch their ass when they're thinking. Because that's where their brain is.

—*Tim Allen*

Toilet

Dogs are gross, they drink out of the toilet. But when you're going to the bathroom, maybe your dog is thinking, "Hey, hey, hey! I drink out of that thing! Why don't you just go in my dish, and save yourself a walk down the hallway?"

—*Garry Shandling*

A man in Washington has invented a new briefcase that turns into a portable toilet. Which means that now, the guy sitting next to you on the train using his cell phone won't seem so bad.

—*Conan O'Brien*

I installed a bunch of low-flow toilets in my house to conserve water. But it's not working out, my dog is dying of dehydration.

—Wally Wang

Toys

Remember the lawn dart? This was perfectly acceptable when we were kids. "Hey, what should we do with this piece of plastic with a six-inch, razor-edge pointy metal shaft? Let's have the kids heave them at each other." "What if they lose an eye?" "Hell, they have two. Let the little one-eyed bastards play!"

—Elvira Kurt

I realized that commercials were misleading when I was a little kid. Like the Power Wheels ads that showed a five-year-old spinning through the mud having a great time. It failed to mention that these things went two miles an hour. Your friends walked faster than you, and you were flooring the thing. "Wait up . . . *vrooooom* . . . wait up!"

—Dominic Dierkes

I didn't get a toy train like the other kids. I got a toy subway instead. You couldn't see anything, but every now and then you'd hear this rumbling noise go by.

—Steven Wright

Transportation

If you're ever feeling low, just take a saunter over to the local bus station, and you'll perk right up. It looks like a Munster family reunion. There are people with teeth like Indian corn, eyes pointing in different directions, Kentucky Fried Chicken buckets used as luggage. And you know nobody there has ever filled out a long form in their whole lives.

—*Dobie Maxwell*

For a while I didn't have a car, I had a helicopter. No place to park it, so I just tied it to a lamppost and left it running.

—*Steven Wright*

Transvestite

At school I didn't tell the other kids that I was a transvestite. Because I was afraid they'd beat me with sticks. "He said a word we didn't understand! And he won at Scrabble with it!"

—*Eddie Izzard*

Trampoline

I have a trampoline in my backyard. Whenever I'm home, I put on Helen Reddy's "I Am Woman" really loud, and jump. My neighbors think I'm really weird, because they don't know that I have a trampoline. They just know they see me over the fence every few seconds.

—*Paula Poundstone*

TV

I watch the Discovery Channel and you know what I've discovered? I need a girlfriend. And the more Discovery Channel you watch the less chance you ever have of meeting a woman, because it fills your head full of odd facts that can come out at any moment, "Hello, did you know Hitler was ticklish? That the sea otter has four nipples? Don't run away!"

—*Dave Attell*

I find television very educational. Every time someone turns on the set, I go into the other room and read a book.

—*Groucho Marx*

Did you see *Ellen,* the coming out episode? That was a watershed for American television. The ABC affiliate in Birmingham, Alabama, right-wing state, they refused to show it. Instead, they had a Rock Hudson film festival.

—*Norman K.*

Have you noticed that TV families never watch television?

—*Henny Youngman*

With high-definition TV everything looks bigger and wider. Kind of like going to your twenty-fifth high school reunion.

—*Jay Leno*

Who was the guy able to sell *Hogan's Heroes* to a network? "Okay, here's the idea. A group of soldiers held in Nazi prison camp. It's a comedy!" "Hmm, that's interesting. Tell me more." "These soldiers are imprisoned by the Nazis behind barbed wire. And if they try to escape they'll be shot!" "I love it! It's a laff riot!"

—*Gilbert Gottfried*

NBC's TV movie based on the life of Jesus, they couldn't shoot that in L.A. Couldn't find three wise men and a virgin.

—*Jay Leno*

I'm getting tired of very special episodes on TV. Seems like *Little House on the Prairie* started this trend, with another tragedy every week. I think it got canceled because eventually everyone was either deaf, blind, or crushed by a stagecoach.

—*Brock Cohen*

I couldn't find the remote control to the remote control.

—*Steven Wright*

I can't believe that the people on *Jerry Springer* are that clueless. They're on a show titled "I'm Sleeping with My Husband's Brother," and the husband asks, "Baby, is there something you want to tell me?" How stupid can a person be? On the application to be a Springer guest it must say, "Can you read subtitles? No? Come on in, we want you!"

—*Dominic Dierkes*

The worst thing about television is that everybody you see on television is doing something better than what you're doing. You never see anybody on TV just sliding off the front of the sofa, with potato chip crumbs all over their shirt.

—*Jerry Seinfeld*

The cable TV sex channels don't expand our horizons, don't make us better people, and don't come in clearly enough.

—*Bill Maher*

Now they're talking about five hundred channels. I can't wait to see what kind of brilliantly horrific programs are out there when we get up to half a thou. Hey, I'd give the Cat Box Channel a chance if it came with basic cable.

—*Dennis Miller*

One night I walked home very late and fell asleep in somebody's satellite dish. My dreams were showing up on TVs all over the world.

—Steven Wright

UFO

I think that's why the aliens don't ever stay, look at the people they meet. Every time they come here they land in the middle of nowhere, and meet two guys in overalls with no teeth. "C'mere, you little critters. Earl and me would take you bowling, if you had a couple more fingers on you."

—Kathleen Madigan

Unemployment

The problem with unemployment is that the minute you wake up in the morning, you're on the job.

—Slappy White

Unemployment is a tough thing. Even if you get a job, they take unemployment out of your check every week, and show it to you in that little box. How good can it be for your confidence that every paycheck has got the word "unemployment" on it? You can't get it out of your head. You just got the job, they're already getting ready for you to get laid off!

—Jerry Seinfeld

Kmart has announced that it is laying off hundreds of employees. Smart move. Now the only place those people can afford to shop will be Kmart.

—*Johnny Robish*

Vanity

I'm soo obsessive about my looks. I spend a lot of time each day just staring in the mirror. No wonder I get in so many traffic accidents.

—*Tanya Luckerath*

Vegetarian

I've been on a vegetarian diet for three weeks, and never have my houseplants looked so good to me.

—*Daniel Lybra*

I am not a vegetarian because I love animals. I am a vegetarian because I hate plants.

—*A. Whitney Brown*

Vegetables are of less importance than meat. Do you think anyone would really care if lima beans got tangled up in the tuna nets?

—*Gene Perret*

Would you believe that there are people who will shoot heroin but won't eat red meat? They say, "Red meat? That'll kill you." Well, yes, if you put it in a needle and shoot it into your arm. Just the size of the needle alone will kill you.

—*Chris Rock*

Veterinarian

I have such an expensive vet. I go to pick my dog up and the girl behind the counter says, "Three thousand dollars." The whole waiting room looks up. A woman says, "What happened?" "Well, apparently the dog bought a car after I dropped him off."

—*Elayne Boosler*

My veterinarian has an inferiority complex, he only operates on stuffed animals.

—*Johnnye Jones Gibson*

Viagra

Viagra is the work of the devil. Now we girls can look forward to having sex with really old guys, for a really long time. I can see it now. He's screaming, "Who's your granddaddy, who's your granddaddy? I can't remember. What were we doing? Was I enjoying it?"

—*Le Maire*

A Japanese scientist has invented a spray-on Viagra. And if you thought the cosmetics clerks in the mall were annoying before when they spritzed you . . .

—*Jay Leno*

In France, they're considering shipping Viagra to the cathedrals to see if they can straighten out the hunchbacks.

—*Bill Maher*

Video Game

Microsoft announced that they're developing a video game for people who don't have or need computers, but still want to find a way to send money to Bill Gates.

—*Bill Maher*

Weapons

The very existence of flamethrowers proves that some time, somewhere, someone said to themselves, "You know, I want to set those people over there on fire, but I'm just not close enough to get the job done."

—George Carlin

Countries are making nuclear weapons like there's no tomorrow. But maybe instead of trying to build newer and bigger weapons of destruction, we should be thinking about getting more use out of the ones we already have.

—Emo Philips

Wedding

What are the scariest words known to man? "Till death do us part." Why not, "Until my car breaks down?" Or "Until I run out of money?"

—Damon Wayans

I hate being a bridesmaid, because I must dress to the bride's taste. My best friend sent me this black-purple, floor-length dress, two sizes too small. I shuffled down the aisle like the Bridesmaid of Frankenstein. Just wait until I get married. Lucky Charms are my favorite cereal, and you're going as a leprechaun bridesmaid, bitch.

—*Tamara Kastle*

I'm not saying marriage doesn't work for some people. But there are things you must prepare yourself for. The vows are just the beginning. They should have Rod Serling come out during the ceremony and announce, "You are about to take a journey not of sight and sound, to a realm where logic and reason seldom meet. . . . Welcome to the Twilight Zone."

—*Sinbad*

Erik Menendez got married in prison. His parents must be so proud . . . ohhh. I think it was a shotgun wedding.

—*Jay Leno*

Next to hot chicken soup, a tattoo of an anchor on your chest, and penicillin, I consider a honeymoon one of the most overrated events in the world.

—*Erma Bombeck*

I love weddings, but I cry. Because they're not mine.

—*Wendy Liebman*

Weight

I don't know why everybody talks about losing weight. That's an ill-conceived phrase. Fat people never lose weight. They always know right where it is. And dropping a few pounds? I dropped a few pounds last week. They landed around my knees.

—*Louie Anderson*

I lost twenty pounds. Unfortunately, I was in England at the time.

—*Daniel Lybra*

According to a new study, overweight people have a better sex drive than thin people. I think that's because overweight people have to drive a lot further to get sex.

—*Jay Leno*

White Trash

I think of myself lovingly as white trailer trash. My parents recently made up their will. Everything is split equally between me and my sister. She's getting the house, but I'm getting the porch and the wheels.

—*Lynda Montgomery*

Wife

Why does my wife want me to go shopping with her? She knows I'm no good at it. She's going to want to do stuff like try different things on. Soon as she comes out of the dressing room with the first thing on, to me it's like a bank robbery. "Let's go! That's the one! Get in the car! Let's go! Let's go!"

—*Ritch Shydner*

Living with my wife is like taking orders from a drill sergeant. I have to work damn hard to get a weekend pass.

—*Irv Gilman*

With my wife there's always something. The other night I had a fight with the dog. My wife said the dog was right. And she told me this in front of the dog. Now the dog has no respect. My wife throws the ball, he waits for me to bring it back.

—*Rodney Dangerfield*

My wife will wake up, roll over, ask, "What are you doing?" "I'm reading." "I thought we were going to talk to each other." "You fell asleep." "So right away you gotta pick up a book?" She gets mad that I'm not focusing on her, even while she's sleeping. I guess my wife's vision of how life should be is that I pay attention to her at every waking moment, and when she falls asleep I sketch her.

—*Ray Romano*

Women

A new survey shows that the more female you are physically, the harder it is to be taken seriously in business. For example, women with very large breasts have a harder time being promoted than women with penises.

—*Heidi Joyce*

Freud accused women of having penis envy. I have no reason to be jealous of a penis. At least when I get out of the ocean, all my bodily parts are still the same size.

—*Sheila Wenz*

Women now have choices. They can be married, not married, have a job, not have a job, be married with children, unmarried with children. Men have the same choice we've always had: work, or prison.

—*Tim Allen*

A study in the *Washington Post* says that women have better verbal skills than men. I just want to say to the authors of that study: *Duh*.

—Conan O'Brien

When women are depressed they eat or go shopping. Men invade another country. It's a whole different way of thinking.

—Elayne Boosler

If there were no women in the world, men would be naked, driving trucks, living in dirt. Women came along and gave us a reason to comb our hair.

—Sinbad

If women ruled the world and we all got massages, there would be no war.

—Carrie Snow

Work

A survey says that American workers work the first three hours every day just to pay their taxes. So that's why we can't get anything done in the morning; we're government employees!

—Jay Leno

A study came out this week that said one out of four American workers is angry at work. And the other three save it for the loved ones at home.

—*Bill Maher*

In Japan, the highest-paid executive earns only fifteen times what the average worker does. Here, CEOs earn five hundred times more, but that's supposed to motivate the American worker. To do what, kidnap his boss?

—*Norman K.*

No matter how much the boss likes you, if you work in a bank you can't take home samples.

—*Eddie Cantor*

When I worked in the computer industry, people often referred to me as a female executive. Is that necessary? I prefer the more politically correct "salary-impaired."

—*Jackie Wollner*

I used to work in a fire hydrant factory. You couldn't park anywhere near the place.

—*Steven Wright*

When I was a kid I got no respect. I worked in a pet store. People kept askin' how big I'd get.

—*Rodney Dangerfield*

World

Japanese researchers say they have found that the Earth is emitting a constant, very low frequency hum. Asked why the Earth was humming, scientists said it was most likely because the world had forgotten the words.

—*Craig Kilborn*

I'm sitting on top of the world, and I've got hemorrhoids.

—*Rodney Dangerfield*

Wrestling

Minnesota governor Jesse Ventura returned to the wrestling ring to referee the WWF Summer Slam. Before the match Ventura heatedly explained to Stone Cold Steve Austin how the electoral college works. That, and no nut kicks. Ventura's appearance fee of a hundred thousand dollars will go to charities benefiting the people of Minnesota. Especially those who fell into a deep depression after realizing that their drug- and alcohol-induced joke vote actually counted.

—*Jon Stewart*

If professional wrestling did not exist, could you come up with this idea? Could you envision the popularity of huge men in tiny bathing suits, pretending to fight?

—Jerry Seinfeld

Writing

I don't write much fiction, except for this great short story every April 15.

—Norman K.

Wrong Number

Today I dialed a wrong number. The other person said, "Hello?" and I said, "Hello, could I speak to Joey?" They said, "Uh, I don't think so. He's only two months old." I said, "I'll wait."

—Steven Wright

Yoga

They say that yoga is a great way to use your body to reach a higher consciousness. I find it's a lot easier to just drink, to get your legs behind your neck like that.

—Wendy Liebman

Zoo

I was an ugly kid. My father never took me to the zoo. He said, "If they want you, they'll come get you."

—*Rodney Dangerfield*

The San Diego Zoo is trying to breed pandas. They haven't succeeded yet, so to insure insemination, they're going to leave the female panda in a hotel room used by the players of the NBA.

—*Wally Wang*

green room

Natasha Ahanin is an actress and stand-up comedian who has performed at the Comedy Store in Hollywood.

Fred Allen was a classic comedian of vaudeville, Broadway, and movies, and a writer for early television shows, including *The Perry Como Show*.

Tim Allen is the star of the ABC sitcom *Home Improvement* and movies including *Toy Story*.

Woody Allen is a comedian, actor, and Academy Award–winning director of films that include *Annie Hall* and *Mighty Aphrodite*.

Louie Anderson is the host of NBC's *Comedy Showcase* and the new *Family Feud*, and author of the best-selling book *Dear Dad*.

Jack Archey was a CPA who decided that having a steady, well-paying job was drastically overrated and has since performed his comedy at the Comedy Store, the L.A. Comedy Cabaret, and the Hollywood Laugh Factory.

Tom Arnold is a comedian and actor who has appeared in the movies *True Lies* and *Nine Months*.

Atom is an artist, actor, and singer-songwriter whose music will be featured in the movies *Perfect Fit* and *Bar Hopping*, starring Kelly Preston. As a comedian, Atom has performed at the Comedy Store and LunaPark.

Dave Attell has been a writer for *Saturday Night Live*, nominated for an American Comedy Award, and star of his own Comedy Central "Pulp Comics" special.

Willie Barcena is a comedian who has appeared several times on *The Tonight Show*.

Dave Barry is the author of a gadzillion humor books, including *The World According to Dave Barry*.

Todd Barry has starred in his own Comedy Central special.

Joy Behar is a comedian and actress who serves as comic relief on the ABC daytime talk show *The View*.

Richard Belzer is a comedian and the actor who plays Munch on *Homicide* and *Law and Order*, and also hosts *Crime Stories* on Court TV.

Milton Berle is a classic comedian with numberless appearances on *The Ed Sullivan Show* and *The Tonight Show*.

Matina Bevis has performed at a number of women's festivals, including the Southern Women's Festival.

Mike Binder is a comedian, screenwriter, and director of *Blankman, Indian Summer,* and *Crossing the Bridge*.

Erma Bombeck was a housewife and humorist with dozens of best-selling humor books to her credit.

Elayne Boosler has starred in her own HBO and Showtime specials, including "Party of One."

Sue Bova is an actress, comedian, singer, and voice-over and jingle artist for films, television, Internet radio, musical theater, and opera.

Mike Brennan was an award-winning journalist nominated for the Pulitzer Prize who gave it all up to join the circus version of editorials: political comedy.

David Brenner has been in this thing called comedy for nigh on forty years, including appearing on *The Late Show with David Letterman* and *The Tonight Show.*

Gloria Brinkworth is a psychologist and stand-up comedian who has performed at the Comedy Store.

Mel Brooks is a comedian, writer, and director of such films as *Young Frankenstein* and *Blazing Saddles*.

A. Whitney Brown has been a host of "Weekend Update" on *Saturday Night Live* and can also be seen on Comedy Central's *Daily Show.*

Judy Brown is the editor of this book and was also a staff writer for the Showtime sitcom *Sherman Oaks.*

George Burns was a classic comedian whose career stretched from vaudeville to the *Burns and Allen* sitcom and the movie *Oh, God!*

Brett Butler is the star of the now syndicated sitcom *Grace Under Fire.*

Red Buttons is a classic comedian and actor whose films include *Sayonara.*

Eddie Cantor was a comedian whose career stretched from vaudeville to Broadway and the movies, including the show *Banjo Eyes*.

Nick Capallo was featured on Comedy Central's *Comics Come Home*.

Drew Carey is the star of the ABC series *The Drew Carey Show* and *Whose Line Is It Anyway?*

George Carlin has won a Grammy and a CableAce award, and was nominated for an Emmy for his comedy albums and HBO and network comedy specials.

Jim Carrey is the star of movies that range from *Dumb and Dumber* to *The Truman Show* and *Man on the Moon*.

Bea Carroll is a singer-songwriter and comedian who has performed at the Comedy Store, the Cinegrill, and the Jazz Bakery.

Carrot Top fools with props big-time, and it's got him from *The Tonight Show* to his own movie, *Chairman of the Board*.

Johnny Carson hosted NBC's *The Tonight Show* for more than thirty years.

Dick Cavett parlayed stand-up comedy into his own talk shows on network television, PBS, and cable.

Cedric the Entertainer is one of the Kings of Comedy Road Show and a costar of *The Steve Harvey Show*.

Fran Chernowsky is a freelance paralegal and stand-up comedian.

Margaret Cho has won an American Comedy Award and starred in her own HBO and Comedy Central specials.

Adam Christing is the president of Clean Comedians and editor of the books *Comedy Comes Clean* and *Comedy Comes Clean II*.

Sarah Citron is an openly gay comedian who has been featured on the TV show and video *In the Life*.

Louis C. K. was featured on Comedy Central's *Young Comedians at Aspen*.

Kate Clinton has released a number of her own comedy albums, been a writer for *The Rosie O'Donnell Show,* and appeared on Comedy Central's *Out There II*.

Jack Coen made a dozen appearances on *The Tonight Show* and, no fools they, they made him a staff writer. He also recently starred in his own Comedy Central special.

Brock Cohen is a screenwriter and stand-up comedian who has performed at the Comedy Store in Hollywood.

Bill Cosby has starred in TV shows that range from *I Spy* to *Cosby* and is the author of several best-selling humor books.

Eileen Courtney is a former TV technical director and current full-time mom who is always funny, and needs to be to keep her sanity.

Billy Crystal is an actor and director of movies that include *City Slickers* and *Mr. Saturday Night,* and host of HBO's *Comic Relief.*

Mark Curry is the star of the syndicated sitcom *Hangin' with Mr. Cooper.*

Rodney Dangerfield has starred in the movies *Caddyshack, Back to School,* and improbably enough, *Natural Born Killers,* and has won a Grammy for his comedy album *No Respect.*

Evan Davis has appeared on *The Tonight Show,* NBC's *Comedy Showcase,* and Showtime's *Comedy Club Network.*

Frank DeCaro is a movie critic for Comedy Central's *Daily Show.*

Ellen DeGeneres was the groundbreaking star of ABC's *Ellen* and has been featured in movies that include *Love Letters* and *Mr. Wrong.*

Lea DeLaria was the host of Comedy Central's *Out There* and has appeared on Broadway in *On the Town* and *The Most Fabulous Story Ever Told.*

Dominic Dierkes is a fifteen-year-old high school student and stand-up comedian who has performed at the Loony Bin in Memphis, Tennessee.

Jeannie Dietz has written jokes for Joan Rivers.

Phyllis Diller is a classic comedian who has appeared in a number of movies and dozens of TV shows, including *The Tonight Show.*

Joe Ditzel is a comedian with a weekly humor column syndicated on the Web by iSyndicate at www.joeditzel.com and editor of the book *Best of the Net Wits.*

Beth Donahue is the author of the humor book *This Is Insanity!: No Dieting, No Exercising, No Counseling, No Results: Stay the Way You Look and Feel—Forever.*

Rick Ducommun has appeared on *Evening at the Improv,* VH-1's *Spotlight,* and in the movies *Neighbors* and *Groundhog Day.*

Dwight is a Los Angeles actor and comedian who has been seen on MTV's *Johnny Rotten Show.*

Jeffrey Essmann is a New York performance artist and comedian.

Bob Ettinger has appeared on *Evening at the Improv,* and Showtime's *Comedy Club Network.*

Mitch Fatel has played a comedian patient on Comedy Central's *Dr. Katz, Professional Therapist.*

Hugh Fink has been a writer for *Saturday Night Live* and has starred in his own Comedy Central special.

Greg Fitzsimmons has been featured on *The Late Show with David Letterman* and at the Montreal Comedy Festival.

Jeff Foxworthy is known both for his former eponymous sitcom and *You Might Be a Redneck If . . . ,* the biggest-selling comedy album of all time.

Fry and Laurie are a British comedy team best known over here for the PBS series *Jeeves and Wooster.*

Jim Gaffigan has appeared on Comedy Central's *Dr. Katz, Professional Therapist.*

Joey Gallinal is a Cuban-American comedian in the South Florida area who has performed at Uncle Funnies, the Improv, and Rascals comedy club.

Janeane Garofalo is the queen of the alternative comedians and an actress who has appeared in films that include *The Truth About Cats and Dogs* and *Mystery Men.*

Irv Gilman is a political activist and comedian who has performed at the Comedy Store in Hollywood, Comedy on the Edge in Sherman Oaks, and the Northwoods Inn in Big Bear.

Jackie Gleason was a comedian and actor who starred in movies that included *The Hustler* and *Papa's Delicate Condition,* and the classic 1950s sitcom *The Honeymooners.*

Whoopi Goldberg is center square on *Hollywood Squares* and host of *Comic Relief.* She also hosted the Oscars and won an Oscar for her role in the movie *Ghost.*

Bobcat Goldthwait has starred in the movies *Scrooged* and *Shakes the Clown,* and on TV series that include the syndicated sitcom *Unhappily Ever After* and *Bobcat's Big Ass Show* on FX.

Marga Gomez has been featured on Comedy Central's *Out There in Hollywood.*

Gilbert Gottfried has been featured in the movie *Problem Child* and as the voice of the parrot in *Aladdin.*

Sue Grafton is one of our favorite witty mystery writers, with an alphabetic series of novels to her credit. But, hey, that's a funny line she wrote, and we quoted her.

Robin Greenspan has been featured on Comedy Central's *Out There in Hollywood.*

E. L. Greggory is a regular at the Comedy Store in Hollywood.

Gypsy Rose Lee was a humorist and ecdysiast, best known for being funny while removing her clothes.

Arsenio Hall was the host of *The Arsenio Hall Show* (do I hear an echo?) and featured in the movie *Coming to America.*

Steve Harvey is the host of *It's Showtime at the Apollo* and the star of UPN's *The Steve Harvey Show.*

Mitch Hedberg, winner of the Seattle Comedy Competition, has appeared on *The Late Show with David Letterman,* *The Conan O'Brien Show,* and his own Comedy Central special.

Tom Hertz has been a featured patient on Comedy Central's *Dr. Katz, Professional Therapist.*

Stephanie Hodge is the star of the syndicated sitcom *Unhappily Ever After.*

Daryl Hogue is a comedian and voice-over talent who has been featured in commercials for 7-Eleven, Ford, and Hewlett-Packard.

Bob Hope is a classic comedian whose career has ranged from vaudeville to a series of road movies with Bing Crosby and innumerable television specials.

Coincidentally enough, **D. L. Hughley** is the star of the ABC sitcom *The Hughleys*.

Warren Hutcherson has starred in his own HBO half hour comedy special, been featured at the Aspen Comedy Festival, and was a producer of the sitcom *Living Single*.

Shannon Ireland is a comedian based in Bloomington, Indiana, who performs at midwestern comedy clubs, church groups, hospital auxiliary banquets, homeless kitchen holiday dinners, and anywhere else that'll have her.

Eddie Izzard is the British transvestite and stand-up comedian who starred in his own 1999 HBO special—we don't have to be more specific than that, do we?

Jeff Jena has appeared on *Evening at the Improv*, Showtime's *Comedy Club Network*, and Comedy Channel's *Make Me Laugh*.

Jake Johannsen starred in his own HBO *One Night Stand* and was nominated for an American Comedy Award.

Johnnye Jones Gibson works for a newspaper, freelances as a journalist, and writes screenplays.

Heidi Joyce has appeared on the CBS special "Everybody Loves Raymond's Ray Day" and opened for Melissa Manchester in Las Vegas.

Norman K. (normank.comic@usa.net) is a comedian who's been a regular at the Improv in New York. He's also a journalist and a licensed New York City tour guide.

Corey Kahane has appeared on Lifetime's *Girls Night Out*, Comedy Central, and NBC's *Comedy Showcase*.

Jann Karam has appeared on *Politically Incorrect, The Tonight Show, Evening at the Improv,* and Lifetime's *Girls Night Out.*

Tamara Kastle is an actress and comedian who has appeared on Comedy Central and *The Tonight Show.*

Jonathan Katz plays the doctor on Comedy Central's *Dr. Katz, Professional Therapist.*

Max Kauffman was a classic comedian who performed on *The Tonight Show.*

Garrison Keillor is a writer and humorist best known for his book *Lake Wobegon Days.*

Maura Kennedy is an actress and comedian who has appeared on the sitcom *Cybill,* is a recurring character on *Days of Our Lives,* and was a finalist in the World Championship of Performing Arts, but didn't win Ben Stein's money on Comedy Central.

In addition to being the Comedy Queen of Sardonica, **Laura Kightlinger** is one of Comedy Central's *Pulp Comics.*

Jean Kerr was a humor writer best known for her book *Please Don't Eat the Daisies.*

Craig Kilborn is the host of CBS's *The Late Late Show.*

Brian Kiley has appeared on Comedy Central's *Dr. Katz, Professional Therapist.*

Andy Kindler has appeared on *The Late Show with David Letterman* and was the host of Animal Planet's *Pet Shop.*

Robert Klein is a comedian who has segued from best-selling 1970s comedy albums to performing in a number of movies, including *The Landlord,* and a recurring role on the TV series *Sisters.*

Dr. Brian Koffman is a comedian and doctor with a family practice in Southern California who loves to laugh and joke with his patients, and comedy audiences.

Jared Krichevsky is an eighteen-year-old actor on the stage and in commercials, both radio and TV, as well as a comedian who has performed at the Comedy Store.

Elvira Kurt has starred in her own Comedy Central special.

Cathy Ladman has appeared on *The Tonight Show* a bazillion times, is a recurring neighbor on *Caroline in the City*, and has also appeared on *Just Shoot Me*.

Denis Leary has starred in his own HBO specials and a number of films, including *The Ref* and *Two If by Sea*.

Okay, she's not a comedian, but **Fran Lebowitz** is the incisively witty author of best-selling humor books including the recently released *The Fran Lebowitz Reader* and the upcoming *Exterior Signs: Health*.

Robert G. Lee can be seen on the religious game show *Inspiration, Please* on the Faith and Values network.

James Leemer has appeared on Comedy Central's *Dr. Katz, Professional Therapist*.

Thyra (tear-ah) **Lees-Smith** lives in Los Angeles and performs in many local clubs, including the Comedy Store.

Carol Leifer was a producer on *Seinfeld* and the star of her own series, *Alright Already*.

Le Maire has opened for Caroline Rhea's summer tour, been featured at the Toyota Comedy Festival, and performed on Comedy Central's *Make Me Laugh*.

Jay Leno is the host of NBC's *The Tonight Show*.

David Letterman is the host of CBS's *The Late Show with David Letterman*.

In addition to his numerous HBO specials, **Richard Lewis** has starred in the sitcom *Anything but Love* and in the Mel Brooks movie *Robin Hood: Men in Tights*.

Wendy Liebman has appeared on *The Tonight Show* and in her own HBO comedy special, and won an American Comedy Award.

Joel Lindley has appeared on Comedy Central's *Make Me Laugh*.

Shirley Lipner is a comedian who was the warm-up for the TBN shows *Rocky Road*, *Safe at Home*, and *Down to Earth*.

S. Rachel Lovey has appeared on Comedy Central and Fox's *Sunday Funnies*, has opened for B. B. King and Big Bad Voodoo Daddy, and is the founder and host of the showcase *Women in Comedy Who Don't Have Their Own Series . . . Yet* at the Comedy Store.

Al Lubel has performed on *Evening at the Improv* and *Comic Strip Live,* and been a featured patient on Comedy Central's *Dr. Katz, Professional Therapist.*

Tanya Luckerath is a comedian and actress who has appeared in the movie *Beg, Borrow and Steel* and the TV comedy show *Clip Joint,* and performed at the Comedy Store in Hollywood.

Mark Lundholm has taken his "twelve-step comedy" to comedy clubs and detox centers across the country, including the Betty Ford Center.

Daniel Lybra is a Roundtable Comedy Conference award-winning comedian and comedy writer.

Danny McWilliams was a cofounder of the group Funny Gay Males and is coauthor of the book *Growing Up Gay.*

Kathleen Madigan won an American Comedy Award for Best Female Stand-up and starred in her very own HBO comedy half hour.

Bill Maher is a comedian and host of ABC's *Politically Incorrect.*

Howie Mandel has been a star of the TV series *St. Elsewhere,* the creator of his own animated series, *Bobby's World,* and host of *The Howie Mandel Show.*

Vince Maranto is a comedian from Chicago who has the distinction of having had two only jobs in his life, McDonald's and comedy. He was the manager of what at one time was the world's busiest McDonald's. He is currently developing a drive-through window for comedy clubs.

Mark Maron has appeared on Comedy Central's *Comics Come Home.*

Steve Martin is a comedian who has starred in or directed comedy films from *The Jerk* to *Bowfinger.*

Groucho Marx was a comedian who, with the Marx Brothers, made a number of the funniest films of the 1930s, including *Duck Soup,* and whose marvelous 1950s quiz show, *You Bet Your Life,* still deserves viewing on some cable channel smart enough to feature it.

Jackie Mason is a forty-year comedy veteran and the star of several one-man Broadway shows, including *The World According to Me*.

Dobie Maxwell (Mr. Lucky) has been taking life's lumps since birth. Almost famous, he is a comedy club headliner and a morning radio host, and teaches comedy classes nationwide.

Frank Maya has been featured on Comedy Central and the PBS series *In the Life*.

Kevin Meaney is the host of the Animal Planet series *You Lie Like a Dog*.

H. L. Mencken was an American writer, editor, journalist, and wit whose books include *The Charlatanry of the Learned* and *A Book of Burlesques*.

John Mendoza has appeared on a number of television shows, including *Evening at the Improv, The Tonight Show*, and his very own sitcom.

Cathryn Michon is a stand-up comedian who stars in *The Grrl Genius Club Show* at the Hollywood Improv. She has written for a number of TV series and is the author of the book *The Grrl Genius Guide to Life*.

Bette Midler is a comedy diva who has appeared in movies from *Beaches* to *The First Wives Club*.

Dennis Miller is the possessor of a God-given sarcasm and the star of HBO's *The Dennis Miller Show*.

Lynda Montgomery has appeared on VH-1's *Spotlight* but considers the highlight of her career to be her performance at the 1993 March on Washington in front of an audience of one million people.

Martin Mull is a comedian and actor whose TV appearances range from *The Smothers Brothers Comedy Hour* and *The Tonight Show* to the role of the gay boss on *Roseanne*.

Sue Murphy was the star of her own Comedy Central special.

Robert Murray is an aerospace engineer and a stand-up comedian.

Rebecca Nell is an actress, writer, and comedian who has performed at a number of L.A. clubs, including the Comedy Store.

Bob Newhart is a comedian who has had several sitcoms named after him, and for good reason.

green room

Conan O'Brien, a former writer for *Saturday Night Live* and *The Simpsons,* is now the host of the NBC talk show *Late Night with Conan O'Brien.*

Rosie O'Donnell is the star of the cheery talk show *The Rosie O'Donnell Show* and has been featured in movies that include *Sleepless in Seattle* and *Exit to Eden.*

Despite her humble origins in the rubber capital of Akron, Ohio, **Ann Oelschlager** has risen to great success in the City of Angels, where she lives in an apartment building with a swimming pool.

P. J. O'Rourke is a humorist, satirist, and author of books that include *Modern Manners* and *Eat the Rich.*

Patton Oswalt has been seen on *Seinfeld* and is a cast member of CBS's *King of Queens.*

Guy Owen is a comedian who has performed at the Comedy Store, for President and Mrs. Carter, and in commercials for Honda and Black & Decker.

Dorothy Parker was a humorist, short story writer, and screenwriter whose credits included the original *A Star Is Born.*

Nancy Jo Perdue is a stand-up comedian and Seattle-based journalist.

Gene Perret has written jokes for Bob Hope since 1969, won three Emmys and a Writers Guild Award for his TV comedy, and written twenty-five books on humor, including *Comedy Writing Step by Step.*

Emo Philips has appeared on numerous HBO and Showtime specials, as well as in the Weird Al Yankovich movie *UHF.*

John Pinette has appeared on Comedy Central's *Dr. Katz, Professional Therapist.*

Monica Piper has had her own Showtime special, *Only You, Monica,* and has written for *Roseanne.*

Kevin Pollack has starred in movies that include *A Few Good Men* and *The Usual Suspects,* and is the star of the CBS sitcom *Work with Me.*

Brenda Pontiff costarred on the sitcom *The Five Mrs. Buchanans* and has performed as a comedian at the Improvisation, the Comedy Store, and the Laugh Factory.

Paula Poundstone has starred in a number of her own HBO comedy specials and is one of the starring voices on the UPN series *Home Movies*.
In addition to having been one of the frightfully inventive stars of Comedy Central's *Whose Line Is It Anyway?* **Greg Proops** is also the host of their game show *Vs.*

Paul Provenza starred on the last season of *Northern Exposure* and in his own HBO, Showtime, and Comedy Central shows and series.

Richard Pryor is a thirty-year veteran of comedy recording, movies, and TV, including the groundbreaking 1970s *Richard Pryor Show* and the movie *Silver Streak*.

Colin Quinn is host of "Weekend Update" on *Saturday Night Live*.

Gilda Radner was one of the stars of the original cast of *Saturday Night Live*.

Brian Regan has appeared on Comedy Central's *Dr. Katz, Professional Therapist*.

Paul Reiser is the star of the syndicated sitcom based on his marriage, *Mad About You*.

Jim Rez is a Los Angeles–based caterer and comedian.

Caroline Rhea isn't a witch, but she plays one on ABC's *Sabrina, the Teenage Witch*.

Call out the coincidence police—**Tom Rhodes** was the star of the NBC sitcom *Mr. Rhodes*.

Karen Ripley has been performing as an out lesbian since 1977.

Joan Rivers is a comedian, actress, talk show host, and best-selling author.

Denise Munro Robb has appeared on A&E's *Comedy on the Road*.

Johnny Robish is a comedian whose jokes appear frequently in the "Laugh Lines" column of the *Los Angeles Times* and whose "Giggle Bytes" are featured on the Internet radio program *Radio Free OZ*.

Chris Rock is a comedian and actor who is, natch, host of HBO's *Chris Rock Show*.

Paul Rodriguez starred in the sitcom *AKA Pablo,* on numerous HBO specials, and on *Comic Relief.*

Will Rogers was an American humorist whose career spanned from the Ziegfield Follies to the movies.

Kenny Rogerson has appeared on Comedy Central's *Comics Come Home.*

Ray Romano is the star of the ABC series *Everybody Loves Raymond* and the author of the best-selling book *Everything and a Kite.*

Roseanne is the comedian who has specialized in eponymous TV series, like *Roseanne,* the sitcom, and *The Roseanne Show.*

Mike Rowe was a featured patient on Comedy Central's *Dr. Katz, Professional Therapist* and has appeared on NBC's *Comedy Showcase.*

Jerry Rubin is the funniest political activist in Los Angeles.

Rita Rudner has appeared on *The Tonight Show* and been featured on any number of comedy specials, including her own on HBO.

Mark Russell is the political satirist and songwriter who appears most frequently on PBS.

Bob Saget has been the star of the sitcom *Full House* and host of *America's Funniest Home Videos.*

Robert Schimmel's Warner Bros. CD is *Robert Schimmel Comes Clean.*

Stephanie Schiern is a lawyer and a stand-up comedian who has performed at the Comedy Store.

Lew Schneider has appeared on *Dr. Katz, Professional Therapist.*

Jerry Seinfeld helped rethink the sitcom with his eponymous *Seinfeld.*

Liz Sells is a breast-cancer survivor and stand-up comedian.

Ronnie Shakes was a classic comic who made frequent appearances on *The Tonight Show.*

Garry Shandling was the star and creator of HBO's *Larry Sanders Show.*

Rondell Sheridan was the star of the sitcom *Minor Adjustments* while it made the minor adjustment of switching from ABC to UPN and has been featured on the Nickelodeon series *Uncle Skeeter.*

green room

Ritch Shydner is a comedian who has written for the ABC sitcom *Roseanne* and starred in his own HBO comedy special.

Sarah Silverman has appeared in *Something About Mary*, played a comedy writer on HBO's *Larry Sanders Show*, and been a comedy writer for *Saturday Night Live*.

Sinbad is the star of the movies *Houseguest* and *First Kid*, and the HBO movie *The Cherokee Kid*, as well as several HBO comedy specials.

Brad Slaight has segued from the recurring role of Izzy Adams on *The Young and the Restless* to stand-up comedy.

Tommy Sledge has performed on *Evening at the Improv*, VH-1's *Spotlight*, and *Comic Strip Live*, published a book titled *Kiss It or Die*, and is heard on his syndicated radio program, *Tommy Sledge's Mystery Minute*.

Bob Smith, one of the first openly gay male comics on TV, has performed on *The Tonight Show* and is the author of the book *Openly Bob*.

Margaret Smith is a comedian and sitcom writer who has won an American Comedy Award and was recently featured in her own Comedy Central special.

Tracy Smith has appeared on MTV's *Half-Hour Comedy Hour*, and Lifetime's *Girls Night Out*.

Carrie Snow has appeared on at least a dozen cable comedy shows, and was a staff writer for both *Roseanne* and *The Roseanne Show*.

Dana Snow has been doing stand-up for centuries, and his comedy writing ranges from jokes for Phyllis Diller and other comedians to the Flintstones children's books. Two of his movie scripts are currently optioned, including one based on a joke he wrote for Billy Crystal and the 1997 Academy Awards Show.

David Spade is a star of the sitcom *Just Shoot Me* and the magnum opus *Lost and Found*.

Barry Steiger has opened on the road for Brett Butler, and appeared on the sitcom *Grace Under Fire* and *The Joan Rivers Show*.

David Steinberg is a classic comedian with a Grammy-nominated comedy album and is a director of comedy television shows and films, including *The Wrong Guy, Going Berserk,* and *Paternity.*

Jon Stewart is the host of Comedy Central's *Daily Show.*

Jeff Stilson has appeared on *The Late Show with David Letterman* and is featured on the fourteenth HBO *Young Comedians Show.*

Brad Stine has appeared on *Evening at the Improv* and Showtime's *Comedy Club Network* and is available through Clean Comedians booking agency.

Steven Sweeney has starred in Comedy Central's *Comics Come Home* and in his own HBO special.

Wanda Sykes-Hall has been featured in her own Comedy Central Presents special and is a writer-producer for HBO's *Chris Rock Show.*

In addition to founding her own religion (Judyism), **Judy Tenuta** is a panelist on *The Match Game* and star of the film *Butch Camp.*

Lily Tomlin was an original cast member of *Laugh-In,* has starred in several films, including *Nashville,* and most recently costarred on *Murphy Brown.*

Aisha Tyler has appeared on NBC's *Comedy Showcase.*

Robin Tyler's 1978 comedy album, *Always a Bridesmaid, Never a Groom,* was her third album but her first as an openly lesbian comic. In 1979 she became the first openly gay comedian to appear on national television.

Jeff Valdez has been featured on *Comedy Compadres.*

Jennifer Vally is a Los Angeles–based comedian and host of her own cable access talk show.

Matt Vance is the morning show producer for *Mick & Allen's Freak Show* on Rock 99 radio in Salt Lake City.

Rich Voss has appeared on Comedy Central's *Make Me Laugh.*

Lesley Wake is a comedian, writer, and teacher.

Wally Wang is a comedian and actor who, in his latest performance on the Internet, managed to convince thousands of men that he's actually a twenty-three-year-old blonde. He has also appeared on A&E's *Evening at the Improv,* performs in Las Vegas, wrote the books *Visual Basic for Dummies* and *Microsoft Office for Dummies,* and publishes a computer humor column in *Boardwatch Magazine.*

Joel Warshaw has performed for his family and friends for years, and can now also be seen performing in Los Angeles at the Comedy Store and at the L.A. Cabaret Comedy Club.

Damon Wayans was the star and one of the creators of *In Living Color,* and has starred in several movies, including *The Last Boy Scout,* and three of his own HBO specials.

Cindee Weiss has performed at the NY Comedy Club, the Comedy Cellar, Gotham Comedy Club, Stand-Up NY, and Yuk Yuk's in Toronto.

Sheila Wenz has appeared on Lifetime, A&E, and Comedy Central.

Suzanne Westenhoefer was the star of her own HBO special, "Nothing in My Closet but My Clothes."

Slappy White was a classic comedian, once partnered with Redd Foxx, who went on to perform on *The Ed Sullivan Show, The Tonight Show,* and *Sanford and Son.*

Danny Williams has been an openly gay performer since the early 1980s, when he recorded *Castro Boy,* which sold 30,000 copies.

Karen Williams is an openly gay comedian who has been featured on the video *In the Life.*

Robin Williams received an Academy Award for *Good Will Hunting* and is the Academy Award–nominated star of *Mrs. Doubtfire* and *Flubber,* as well as a cohost of HBO's *Comic Relief.*

Flip Wilson was the star of the 1960s television show *The Flip Wilson Show,* still running on cable.

P. G. Wodehouse was a British humorist and author of a bouquet of novels featuring the indomitable butler Jeeves as hero.

Dennis Wolfberg was a beloved 1980s comedian who was a *Tonight Show* regular and a cast member of the TV series *Quantum Leap.*

Jackie Wollner was a finalist in the prestigious San Francisco Comedy Competition and is the creator of *You Animal You—A One Mammal Show.*

Steven Wright has appeared on numerous HBO specials, was a recurring cast member of *Mad About You,* and received an Oscar nomination for Best Short Film.

Jim Wyatt is a stand-up comedian and animation producer of *Garfield* and *The Twisted Tales of Felix the Cat.*

Henny Youngman was a classic comedian and king of the one-liners whose career ranged from vaudeville and the Catskills to Johnny Carson's *The Tonight Show.*

Kate Zannoni, when she's not in a carpool, camping with the Cub Scouts, or serving Pop-Tarts for dinner, is a stand-up comic in Cleveland, Ohio. To keep her sanity she also performs with other whacked-out women in "Jest the Girls with Big Wits."